Cambridge Elements ≡

Elements in Crime Narratives
edited by
Margot Douaihy
Emerson College
Catherine Nickerson
Emory College of Arts and Sciences
Henry Sutton
University of East Anglia

CRIME FICTION AND ECOLOGY

From the Local to the Global

Nathan Ashman
University of East Anglia

T0323921

CAMBRIDGE
UNIVERSITY PRESS

Shaftesbury Road, Cambridge CB2 8EA, United Kingdom

One Liberty Plaza, 20th Floor, New York, NY 10006, USA

477 Williamstown Road, Port Melbourne, VIC 3207, Australia

314–321, 3rd Floor, Plot 3, Splendor Forum, Jasola District Centre, New Delhi – 110025, India

103 Penang Road, #05–06/07, Visioncrest Commercial, Singapore 238467

Cambridge University Press is part of Cambridge University Press & Assessment, a department of the University of Cambridge.

We share the University's mission to contribute to society through the pursuit of education, learning and research at the highest international levels of excellence.

www.cambridge.org
Information on this title: www.cambridge.org/9781009539319

DOI: 10.1017/9781009358613

First published 2025

A catalogue record for this publication is available from the British Library

ISBN 978-1-009-53931-9 Hardback
ISBN 978-1-009-35863-7 Paperback
ISSN 2755-1873 (online)
ISSN 2755-1865 (print)

Cambridge University Press & Assessment has no responsibility for the persistence or accuracy of URLs for external or third-party internet websites referred to in this publication and does not guarantee that any content on such websites is, or will remain, accurate or appropriate.

Crime Fiction and Ecology

From the Local to the Global

Elements in Crime Narratives

DOI: 10.1017/9781009358613
First published online: January 2025

Nathan Ashman
University of East Anglia
Author for correspondence: Nathan Ashman, n.ashman@uea.ac.uk

Abstract: This Element examines how contemporary ecological crime narratives are responding to the scales and complexities of the global climate crisis. It opens with the suggestion that there are certain formal limits to the genre's capacity to accommodate and interrogate these multifaceted dynamics within its typical stylistic and thematic bounds. Using a comparative methodological approach that draws connections and commonalities between literary crime texts from across a range of geographical locales – including Asia, Europe, Africa, South America, North America and Oceana – it therefore seeks to uncover examples of world crime fictions that are cultivating new forms of environmental awareness through textual strategies capable of conceiving of the planet as a whole. This necessitates a movement away from considering crime fictions in the context of their distinct and separate national literary traditions, instead emphasising the global and transnational connections between works.

Keywords: ecocriticism, crime fiction, global, environmental humanities, world literature

ISBNs: 9781009539319 (HB), 9781009358637 (PB), 9781009358613 (OC)
ISSNs: 2755-1873 (online), 2755-1865 (print)

Contents

Introduction: Ecological Crime Fiction – From the Local to the Global

At the opening of Ross Macdonald's *Sleeping Beauty* (Macdonald, 1973), protagonist and private detective Lew Archer peers out of the window of a commercial airliner as it approaches the city of Los Angeles, catching his first glimpse of a catastrophic oil spill spanning several miles across the vast coastlines of the fictional Pacific Point. Located towards the windward end of the slick is a ruptured offshore oil platform, described as protruding from the water 'like the metal hand of a dagger that had stabbed the world and made it spill black blood' (1). The violent, somatic imagery that Macdonald employs is immediately striking, situating the spill not as the site of a tragic industrial accident but as the scene of an ecological crime. The resulting fallout – including the spill's disastrous impact on the local flora and fauna of Pacific Point – will hold a central presence as the narrative progresses, intersecting with the text's second and more ostensive mystery: the murder of a man discovered face down in the oily shallows of the coastal surf. Although Archer will eventually connect both crimes back to the buried transgressions and traumas of the corrupt Lennox family – the dynastic owners of the oil company directly responsible for the blowout – the denouement of the novel only partially resolves the environmental crimes that it presents. Fires rage across the polluted shorelines in the closing pages, as the slick continues to resist the totalising structures of the detective novel form. Moreover, Macdonald will disperse accountability beyond the text's immediate criminal agitators, implicating a wider and burgeoning capitalist society of which both detective and reader are part. As freelance reporter Wilbur Cox tells Archer when discussing the corporate brinkmanship that precipitated the spill: 'they're not the only gamblers ... we're all in the game. We all drive cars and we're all hooked on oil. The question is how we can get unhooked before we drown in the stuff' (112).

Whilst this sense of shared guilt constitutes a central facet of the identifiably dark and pessimistic moral vision frequently expounded in the worlds of noir and hard-boiled fiction, it is one that also speaks powerfully to the uncertainty of our current ecological moment. Timothy Morton (2016) is one of several scholars who, in recent times, has drawn a comparison between the 'darkness of ecological awareness' and the 'darkness of noir', pointing to a certain dissonance that accompanies all critical thinking about anthropogenic climate change. In the same way that the noir or hard-boiled protagonist becomes 'implicated' in the narrative's criminal world, ecological awareness forces the contemporary subject into a similarly 'strange loop' where they must confront their own dialectical position as both perpetrator and victim. As Morton (2016) puts it: 'I'm the detective and the criminal!' (9). Morton's employment of the language of crime fiction is suggestive here and points not only to the potential for crime writing to articulate responses to the climate crisis but also to the value of reassessing the mode's traditions, conventions and forms for the ways they might yield new and enlightening perspectives on the entangled global histories of the anthropocene. Ross Macdonald's work is noteworthy in this sense, particularly for the way it redirects the generic atmosphere and poetics of the hard-boiled mode towards an explicit environmental critique. It is unsurprising, then, that Macdonald has often been heralded as one of the crime genre's early 'ecological prophets', and it is certainly tempting to pinpoint a work like *Sleeping Beauty* as a prototypal example of a distinct classification or subgenre of ecologically orientated crime fictions (Wagner-Martin, 2012, 154). Yet the text simultaneously raises some significant questions, not only in relation to how we might formally or conceptually define the parameters of this adjunct mode of crime writing but also concerning the crime novel's broader capacity to productively engage with the scales and territorial complexities of environmental harm. To put it another way: what precisely *is* ecological crime fiction? Is it, as Macdonald himself suggests, simply a question of 'subject matter', where existing modes of the crime novel straightforwardly accommodate a set of environmental thematics within their extant structures and styles (Avery & Nelson, 2016, 124)? Or, conversely, does the eco-crime novel take on its own particular narrative shapes and aesthetic forms, and to what extent do these discrete literary arrangements enable or inhibit the expression of its aforementioned environmental apprehensions?

Although the examination of environmental cataclysm and anthropogenic climate change has formed a constitutive part of the fabric of late twentieth and early twenty-first-century artistic production – with 'cli-fi' (climate fiction) emerging as a robust literary and critical field in its own right – the study of ecological crime fiction is, by contrast, still very much in its infancy. Much of this work to date has tended to centre on so-called literary forms of environmental writing, or on what might be loosely categorised as 'arealist' genre modes, such as sci-fi, dystopia and speculative fiction (King, 2021, 1235). The omission of crime narratives is rooted in an ingrained hierarchical distinction between 'serious' and 'popular' art forms, particularly the assumption that certain types of writing are necessarily constrained by their appeal to established traditions or conventions. Axel Goodbody and Adeline Johns-Putra (2019) make this point explicitly in their book *Cli-Fi: A Companion*, arguing that when the intrigue of a novel 'resides mainly in its status within a particular genre', it can subsequently 'circumscribe readers' understanding of potential solutions to the problems it presents' (4). Here Goodbody and Johns-Putra question the capacity of certain forms of genre fiction to operate outside of their stylistic and thematic dimensions, a limitation that, they argue, might subsequently forestall the reader's critical engagement. Implied here is the assumption that genre fiction serves only to exacerbate, rather than remedy, what Amitav Ghosh (2016) has described as the 'imaginative and cultural failure that lies at the heart of the climate crisis' (8). While Ghosh is largely critical of the 'grid of literary forms' associated with 'serious fiction' (rather than genre) for their failure to negotiate the torrents of the climate crisis, he offers little suggestion that popular forms of writing are any better equipped to tackle this broad representational crisis (8).

As Lucas Hollister (2019) notes, there are certainly persuasive reasons to be sceptical about the crime novel's capacity to account for the scalar complexities of ecological crisis within its limited 'frames of intelligibility' (1012). Many conventional iterations of the genre are typically bound by fairly circumscribed 'temporal and spatial dimensions' and tend to rely on 'definitions of violence that are not necessarily compatible with or useful to contemporary ecocritical thought' (1012). This is particularly problematic when it comes to representing the forms of 'slow violence' most commonly associated with climate change, where it 'occurs gradually, and out of sight .... [and] is dispersed across time and space' (Nixon, 2011, 2). This has not prevented a growing number of scholars from turning their attention to the crime mode's so-called generic features, examining how its conventions may in fact open up (rather than prohibit) 'opportunities to reflect on the forms and functions of environmental criticism and ecological narratives' (Walton & Walton, 2018, 3). Pinpointing the origins of a particular literary or critical tradition is no easy endeavour and the inherent permeability of genres and modes means that the writing and study of ecological crime fiction likely has a longer and more entangled genealogy that can be adequately outlined here. Nonetheless, Patrick D. Murphy's *Ecocritical Explorations in Literary and Cultural Studies* (Murphy, 2009) is often cited as a key source text in the study of ecological crime narratives. In it he calls on literary critics to look more closely at 'nature-oriented mystery novels', those 'with or without detectives and perhaps even without murders', in order to better comprehend the 'degree to which environmental awareness has permeated popular and commercial fiction' (143). Murphy points to the work of Florida crime writers John D. MacDonald and Carl Hiaasen as key examples of a form of mystery fiction that has knowingly and critically taken environmental crime as its subject. Murphy is largely preoccupied with how the crime novel can operate to transmit environmental anxieties to a mass audience, rather than considering what particular forms these narratives take, or the specific ideas that they engage with. Although critics such as Stewart King have latterly dismissed

Murphy's approach for its admittedly limited scope, his work has continued to be referenced by several key scholars, most notably Jo Lindsay Walton and Samantha Walton in their 2018 special issue on 'Crime Fiction and Ecology' for the ecocritical journal *Green Letters*. Walton and Walton bring together a range of essays that 'explore detective fiction in which nature plays a prominent role', as well as other works 'whose ecological themes are latent within ostensibly anthropocentric plotting' (4). In other words, whilst the special issue acknowledges the kind of consciously 'nature-orientated' mysteries that Murphy pinpoints – texts that feature typical genre markers such as the investigator, the criminal and the denouement – it also seeks to extend the field of study to texts that might *unconsciously* lend themselves to ecological interpretations. Sam Walton continues this work in a separate essay, where she stresses the pedagogical importance of bringing crime fiction studies 'into dialogue with ecocriticism [and] the current conditions of our environmental crisis' (Walton & Walton, 2018, 127).

Walton and Walton's special issue remains one of the most significant contributions to the field to date, and suggests two dissimilar (yet not necessarily oppositional) ways of approaching the study of ecological crime fiction: either as a distinctive category of texts with shared formal and/or thematic preoccupations or as a particular mode of interpretation, a way of *reading* genre (Walton & Walton, 2018). The latter is the position broadly taken in my recent collection of essays *The Routledge Handbook of Crime Fiction and Ecology* (Ashman, 2023), which opens up a diverse assemblage of crime narratives from a range of geographical and historical locales to ecocritical perspectives. Whilst the collection certainly contains chapters that analyse 'cognisantly' ecological crime fictions – considering how these fictions are responding to the global climate crisis *now* in the contemporary moment – it also allows for explorations of texts where such anxieties are more thematically latent or contextually situated. It takes the position that all crime fiction is, to some extent, troubled by questions of ecology, not necessarily in the sense of offering a conscious or political interrogation of the relationship between living organisms and the natural world (although some do) but rather as being unavoidably enmeshed in certain historical and ideological understandings of the physical environment. Other critics, however, have been more precise and circumscribed in their theorisations of what constitutes ecological crime fiction, particularly on a formal level. Marta Puxan-Oliva (2020), for instance, attempts to establish eco-crime fiction as something approximating a subgenre, drawing a clear distinction between crime novels where 'environmental issues are marginal' to the story's focus and those where environmental crimes are the 'core problem' (362). Puxan-Oliva is not overly exacting about the particular aesthetic features that unite these new forms but does stress a tendency within such texts to think about 'the planet at large, and about temporal dimensions beyond the individual – and even national – histories that crime fiction has most frequently addressed' (365). Stewart King (2021) takes a similar approach, coining the neologism 'crimate fictions' to refer to a field of texts that 'both narrate the climate catastrophe through the popular conventions of the crime genre and apply the genre's ideological concerns with culpability and criminality to the climate crisis' (1237). King positions crimate fiction as merely 'a subset' of a larger category of 'environmental crime fiction', one that fosters a 'different relationship to place than is evident in many other environmental crime stories' (1239). Within this, he emphasises the need to shift the study of 'environmental' crime fiction away from the localised geographical focus (national/ regional) that has traditionally dominated crime scholarship – such as in essays by Sam Naidu (South Africa; see Naidu, 2014), Linda Haverty Rugg (Scandinavia; see Haverty Rugg, 2017) and Nathan Ashman (California; see Ashman, 2018) – and calls for a broader embracement of comparative and postcolonial theoretical approaches.

Treating 'crimate fiction' as a subgenre in its own right (or, more precisely, a subset of a subgenre) is not without its problems and risks compressing the field of study into a discrete number of actively engaged texts, thus overlooking a more abstracted range of potential ecological considerations. Moreover, such an approach might serve to produce only new forms of chronology and canonisation, further ingraining certain hierarchies and methods of privileging that have historically dogged crime writing and criticism. Where would we begin to pinpoint the origins of such a mode? How would we begin to draw its conceptual boundaries? What would it include or exclude and how might such delimitations serve our aims? These questions aside, Puxan-Olivia's (2020) and King's (2021) respective works are still highly significant for their focus on the contemporary crime novel's particular modes of representation, and how such modes are deployed to better capture the variegated temporal and spatial scales of the climate crisis. In this way, their thinking consciously intersects with a broader 'global turn' in recent crime fiction scholarship, one that has been equally central to environmentalist thought and writing from the mid twentieth century to the present.

'A Sense of Planet': World Crime Fiction and the Imagination of Place

To describe crime fiction as a global literary genre may appear somewhat of a truism. Crime fiction is produced, sold and consumed on a significant scale in almost every country in the world, making it one of the most widely read and universally recognised forms of popular literature. It is the discernibility of its conventions and themes that has no doubt seen it develop into a type of international literary language, one through which specific national or regional examinations of crime, justice and the law can be readily interpreted and understood by a wider global audience. The genre is also highly mobile, consistently crossing borders and moving away from its various centres of production through the mechanisms of international publishing, translation and adaptation. It is this very merging of 'familiar forms' with unfamiliar or 'exotic' content that has become one of the 'major selling points of global crime writing', with crime narratives increasingly emerging as the newest forms of travel literature (Gulddal & King, 2022, 1). As Eva Erdmann (2009) notes: 'On the map of the world there are hardly any areas uncharted by crime fiction, hardly any places that have not yet become the setting for a detective novel' (13). Crime fiction criticism, however, has been comparatively slow in catching up with the genre's global expansion. Scholarship has traditionally tended to substantiate a particular fixed chronology of the genre's historical development, prioritising a foundational canon of Anglo-American texts (typically from writers such as Poe, Doyle, Christie and Chandler) and a particular set of allied literary traditions and forms (such as the locked room mystery and the hard-boiled, police procedural). Subsequent attempts to dismantle this entrenched 'grand narrative' of the genre's development have therefore looked to deprior-itise anglophone literatures, with excellent studies being produced on a variety of crime fiction narratives from competing literary traditions and locales. Whilst such works have certainly been successful in highlighting that the history and development of the genre is more complex and entangled than previous narra-tivisations have suggested, in doing so they have tended to construct 'their own national canons' in a manner not dissimilar from the very 'Anglo American "centre"' they are attempting to dismantle (Stougaard-Nielsen, 2020, 75). In other words, much scholarship remains 'largely committed to the idea of national literatures' and scholars working on such literatures tend not to place them in the context of 'broader global debates' (Gulddal & King, 2022, 3). This is, to a large extent, expressive of the deeper role crime fiction has played in the imagining and cultural construction of place. Formally emerging as a response to the rapid urban and industrial developments of the nineteenth century – as well as to the broader epistemic anxieties of empire – the genre offered its readers new ways of mapping and overcoming the perceived unintelligibility of the modern metropolis. Key to this knowledge production was the figure of the detective, who, through their heightened capacity to interpret material and spatial signs, worked to establish connections between various 'types' of individual, thus 'revealing (and making meaningful for the reader), the social, political, economic, cultural and physical places they inhabit' (King, 2021, 1238). Barbara Pezzotti (2012) therefore positions the sleuth as an evolution of the flâneur, where the 'idler' transmutes into the 'searcher, digging into urban space to find clues beneath the appearance of the metropolitan exterior' (1). Yet, even beyond these specific urban incarnations of the genre, the focus on place, be it the city or the country house, has always been constitutive to crime fiction 'as a locus of meaning' (King, 2021, 1238). In this sense, the crime novel is perhaps the most quintessentially *territorialised* of literary forms, bound, perhaps more than any other, by its typically limited temporal and spatial frames. As such, one might question the extent to which the relative paucity of material on the global crime novel (as a mode or style) is in fact reflective of the crime genre's deeper ties to the histories and machinations of the 'modern, bureaucratic state' (Pepper, 2016, 1). How capable is the crime novel, in other words, of looking beyond the local, particularly if we treat the local as a 'synecdoche of the state' (Pepper & Schmid, 2016, 1)?

Recent crime fiction criticism has endeavoured to contest this dominant focus on local/national traditions, advocating for a more comprehensive understanding of the genre that emphasises postcolonial, transnational and comparative reading practices. In their book *Globalization and the State in Contemporary Crime Fiction* (Pepper & Schmid, 2016), Andrew Pepper and David Schmid argue that 'the production, circulation, and translation' of crime fiction has in fact 'always been an inherently transnational phenomenon' (1). At the same time, they also acknowledge that 'it is only in the last twenty years' that the genre has truly 'mushroomed beyond the familiar scenes of its foundational texts (e.g., London, Paris, New York, Los Angeles)', becoming, in the process, 'a truly global literary genre' (1). The effort to expand knowledge regarding the 'transnational flow of literature in the globalized mediascape of contemporary culture' is continued in the edited collection *Crime Fiction as World Literature* (Nilsson et al., 2017, 2), which examines not only the interplay between the local and the global in contemporary crime narratives but also the 'literary systems' and marketing mechanics that allow for the genre's global distribution and consumption (5). *The Cambridge Companion to World Crime Fiction* (Gulddal et al., 2022) similarly examines the translation and circulation of crime fiction, bringing together texts from around the globe as part of a broader strategy to elucidate 'a new global history of the crime novel' (Gulddal & King, 2022, 21). For two of the editors, Jesper Gulddal and Stewart King, it is the genre's inherent adaptiveness that makes it particularly adept at giving textual shape to the 'interconnectedness of the local, the national and the global that characterises today's world' (Gulddal & King, 2022, 1). These claims are mirrored in *Criminal Moves: Modes of Mobility in Crime*

Fiction (Gulddal et al., 2019), which likewise attempts to offer a new account of the crime novel's history through a reading practice that emphasises elements of mobility and exchange, albeit via a focus on predominantly Western canonical texts. *Transnational Crime Fiction: Mobility, Borders and Detection* (Piipponen et al., 2020b) concerns itself more with the specific social, economic and political repercussions of globalisation and transnationalism, and how these forces have influenced the 'kind of social criticisms crime narratives offer in the contemporary era' (Piipponen et al., 2020a, 3). In a moment where crime is 'increasingly conceptualised as networked and embedded in historical and transcultural contexts', it examines the extent to which crime novels are adapting their particular formal arrangements in order to more accurately conceive of crime that is no longer spatially or temporally delimited (Piipponen et al., 2020a, 3). This focus on the specific impacts of internationalisation and globalisation on contemporary crime writing is shared by *Crime Fiction and National Identities in the Global Age* (J. H. Kim, 2020) and *Investigating Identities: Questions of Identity in Contemporary International Crime Fiction* (Krajenbrink & Quinn, 2009), but with a more specialised emphasis on questions of identity and nationhood.

What unites these works is an attempt to 'deterritorialise' crime writing by replacing the 'traditional Anglocentric understanding' of the genre with a new 'openness to [its] infinite variability' as a global literary form (Gulddal & King, 2022, 22). This rests on a particular type of cosmopolitan/humanist rationale, where deterritorialisation implies the possibility of 'new cultural encounters' by virtue of the 'increasing connectedness of societies around the globe' (Heise, 2008, 10). Through its reach and popularity, crime fiction is thus seen as ideally positioned to map new forms of planetary imagination that move beyond place-based understandings of identity and belonging. Whilst this approach therefore offers a valuable methodological framework through which to establish connections between crime novels from around the globe, what tends to be less clear is how, specifically, the conditions of globalisation have impacted the formal features or narrative arrangements that such texts now employ. What is the 'global' or 'world' crime novel, in other words, and how is it responding to, or mapping, these new transnational complexities within its traditionally territorialised narrative structures?

Here the field of world crime fiction studies can be seen to intersect with a broader debate around globalisation that has dominated social and cultural theory in the last decade, where the very question of 'what cultural and political role attachments to different kinds of space might play, from the local and regional level all the way to the national and global, has assumed central importance' (Heise, 2008, 4–5). This has taken on particular prominence in environmentalist thought and writing, where discourses have 'evolved in a field of tension between the embrace of, and resistance to, global connectedness, and between the commitment to a planetary vision and the utopian reinvestment in the local' (Heise, 2008, 21). Much like the theoretical shift away from national or place-based reading practices that has characterised much of the recent work on world crime fiction, ecocriticism, particularly in the US and the UK, has similarly looked to move on from an 'older-style romantic humanist' tradition that typically focused on the 'local and on retrievals or affirmations of more supposedly "natural" or "ecological" modes of living' (Clark, 2019, 41). This has since been superseded by a new kind of 'green cosmopolitanism', one which tends to emphasise the deeply imbricated scalar relations between the local and the global (Clark, 2019, 41). The transition from local to global perspectives is typified by the work of Ursula K. Heise, who, in her book *Sense of Place and Sense of Planet: The Environmental Imagination of the Global* (2008), emphasises the need to develop a new kind of 'world citizenship' that builds on 'recuperations of the cosmopolitan project in other areas of cultural theory' (10). Without intending to necessarily deny the substantial role that local attachments can play in ongoing environmental discourses, Heise argues that much ecologically orientated thinking has still struggled to reconcile itself with one of the most significant aspects of contemporary understandings of globalisation: 'namely, that the increasing connectedness of societies around the globe entails the emergence of new forms of culture that are no longer anchored in place, in a process that many theorists have referred to as deterritorialisation' (10). Whilst acknowledging that deterritorialisation, particularly when imposed 'from the outside', can precipitate a kind of destructive dislocation and loss that should be rightly apposed, Heise argues that it can simultaneously imply a 'broadening of horizons' that many 'politically progressive movements' have tended to support. For Heise, the continuing challenge for writers and critics is to envision an 'ecologically based advocacy on behalf of the nonhuman world as well as on behalf of greater social environmental justice', one that is centred no longer on a rootedness in local places but 'in ties to territories and systems that are understood to encompass the planet as a whole' (10). It is a critical perspective that shares many commonalties with Laurence Buell's concept of 'ecoglobalism', a 'whole-earth way of thinking and feeling about environmentality' that similarly looks to think beyond nationness, recognising how seldom 'jurisdictional borders correspond to ecological ones' (Buell, 2007, 227).

Given the theoretical proximity between the field of world crime fiction studies and that of contemporary ecocriticism – namely via their shared focus on the meaning and political value of particular forms of spatial attachment – it is surprising how little attention has been paid to environmental or ecological questions in existing critical discourse on the contemporary crime novel, especially in the global context. To date, none of the extended critical works on international, postcolonial or world crime fiction explicitly engage with environmental injustices or climate violence as part of their broader examination of transnational crime and detection. This is all the more notable given that most environmental crimes tend to be eminently global in nature, frequently extending beyond the circumscribed boundaries of the nation-state. Global environmental change and globalisation are, after all, inextricably interlinked, frequently leading to situations of 'double exposure' where those impacted by the negative effects of one process will often simultaneously feel the negative effects of the other (Leichenko and O'Brien, 2008, 4). This critical oversight can, in part, be contextualised in relation to the unique challenge that environmental crime poses to the genre's traditionally constrained spatial, temporal and jurisdictional scope, not to mention its resistance to many existing frameworks of criminality, law and justice. In a moment where much of the world's environmental damage is being undertaken 'legally' by governments and transnational corporations, to what extent does the crime novel need to reconsider ideas such as agency and criminality? How can justice be enacted when criminals are no longer deviant or perverse individuals but abstract, global powers? And how does the crime novel reconcile its conventional drive towards resolution and certainty with the paralysing uncertainty of our future? These are undoubtedly challenging questions, but questions that need to be urgently addressed if we are to bring the study of world crime fiction into a more constructive dialogue with some of the most significant environmental challenges of our time.

Ecological Crime Fiction: From the Local to the Global

As noted, it has been only in shorter critical works by the likes of Stewart King and Marta Puxan-Oliva that the ecological dimensions of global crime fiction (and vice versa) have been scrutinised to a significant degree. For these critics, it is precisely the crime novel's augmenting production and circulation as a form of 'world' literature, not to mention the ostensible capaciousness of its literary forms, that makes it particularly well placed to map and narrate 'the global environmental crisis' (Puxan-Oliva, 2020, 365). Outside of the comparative methodological frameworks that both critics utilise – in contrast to the kind of locally, regionally or nationally situated readings that have tended to dominate ecocritical crime criticism to date – what sets these works apart is their careful consideration of the particular aesthetic blueprints that such crime fictions use, and how these blueprints might 'point to ways of imagining the global that frame localism from a globalist environmentalist perspective' (Heise, 2008, 9). By examining the numerous techniques via which the genre might imagine or theorise 'entangled locations and worlds', they suggest that we can come to a more comprehensive understanding of how crime narratives are collectively responding to the climate crisis on a global scale (Stougaard-Nielsen, 2020, 81). This Element largely seeks to continue the excellent work that has already been undertaken by King and Puxan-Oliva, thinking further about the crime novel's textual strategies for representing the deep enmeshment and interconnectedness of global environmental crises. Yet, unlike these studies – both of which unequivocally assume the crime novel's ability to representationally encompass such entanglements due to its history of geographical mobility and stylistic adaptation – this Element will be far more tentative and circumspect in its approach. Instead, it will follow Andrew Pepper and David Schmid in suggesting that there are certain 'foundational limits' to the capacities of the crime novel to accommodate, and interrogate, the scales and complexities of the global climate crisis within the parameters of its 'most typical form (e.g. a local police detective, or surrogate, investigating a single murder in a particular place)' (2016, 8).

As a prelude to this, Section 1 will examine a selection of local ecological crime fictions, questioning what role these more geographically (and narratively) enclosed texts can still play in producing understandings of, and resistances to, ecological crimes and/or violences that extend beyond the borders of the nation-state. Analysing representations of the carbon economy in novels by Attica Locke and Fernanda Melchor, as well as the relationship between settler colonialism and environmental justice in indigenous crime narratives by Julie Janson and Thomas King, this section emphasises the role of the critic in establishing 'continuities of experience' between fictions that might otherwise be constrained by the boundaries of place, or their particular narrative arrangements (Ghosh, 2016, 62). As such, and irrespective of the types of scalar resistance that the climate crisis poses to the crime novel, these local ecological crime fictions can still contribute meaningfully towards demystifying the opaque global forces that connect places, and lives, across time and space. This relationship between the local and the global constitutes the basis for Section 2, which analyses ecological crime narratives – by writers such as Jassy MacKenzie, Qiu Xiaolong, Antti Tuomainen and Donna Leon – that consciously shift between different spatial scales. Though acknowledging the ways in which these 'glocal' crime narratives 'apply pressure to the traditional features of the genre in an attempt to make it more responsive to a rapidly globalizing world' (Pepper & Schmid, 2016, 12), it suggests that they offer somewhat inert responses to the planetary dynamics they reveal, inhibiting the forms of 'eco-cosmopolitan awareness' that they are able to cultivate (Heise, 2008, 59). Whereas some of these texts express a reconstituted conviction in the power of the state to 'resolve' global eco-capitalist threats or impending environmental disasters, others expose the state's increasing ineffectuality and irrelevancy in the face of these very same pressures. The result is a somewhat stuttering confrontation between two visions of state power, neither of which is wholly successful in articulating forms of cross-cultural or global awareness. Nonetheless, these novels still point to the ways in which ecological crime narratives are attempting to develop new representational forms for conveying a 'sense of planet' (Heise, 2008, 79). The final main section (Section 3) centres on hybridised forms of crime fiction, examining their capacity to generate more expansive ecological visions. Focusing on novels by Gabriela Alemán, Yun Ko-eun, Alexandra Kleeman and Jeff VanderMeer, it will interrogate not only how these texts enlarge the geographical and representational scope of the 'realist' crime novel but also how they disrupt the form's dominant narratological orientation. Indeed, what separates these texts is a movement away from the crime novel's typical concern with questions of guilt. In the process, they commit to radical, yet cautiously optimistic, visions of the future from within the otherwise volatile realities that they present, pushing the crime novel in new and potentially fruitful directions.

Of course, it may well be argued that the very existence of ecological crime fiction (in *any* form) is itself a cause for uncritical celebration, particularly in a world where conservative political forces are continually seeking to invalidate the material reality of the climate crisis. After all, does the genre's framework of villains and victims, its tendency towards closure and resolution, not work to ground and/or humanise the crisis in some way, to make it less opaque and more digestible? Is there not value in this alone, especially given the genre's broad global readership and its particular susceptibility to the sway of market forces? The answer is of course yes, but it is also myopic (perhaps even irresponsible) to argue that simply telling stories – without giving due consideration to *how* we tell them – is enough. Take Michael Crichton's highly successful yet highly paranoid commercial eco-thriller *State of Fear* (Crichton, 2004), in which a cabal of fanatical eco-radicals and self-serving scientists conspire to manufacture climate change for their own ends. The novel has since played a significant role in popularising climate scepticism, with US Senator Jim Inhofe even making the novel required reading for the Senate Committee of

Environment and Public Works, which he chaired between 2003 and 2007 (Trexler, 2015, 35–36). The way we tell stories *does* matter, and it would be a mistake to think that the crime novel need not adapt – formally and thematically – to confront the representational challenges posed by the global climate crisis, or need not rethink the meanings of justice, criminality and law in a world where such terms have taken on new and increasingly complex meanings.

Throughout this Element, I use the term ecological crime fiction not in reference to a subgenre of crime novels with a specific set of conventions or tropes but in allusion to a wider field of texts from across a range of geographical and historical locales, where ecological discourses may be latent, ambient or explicit within their formal and/or thematic content. In this sense, the 'object' of this form of criticism might be better understood as a particular methodological approach, a way of reading genre, rather than a select 'corpus' of literary texts (Heise, 2013, 640). Whilst therefore acknowledging the long genealogy of ecological crime fiction, one that likely stretches back to at least the nineteenth century, this Element focuses exclusively on contemporary (post-millennial) texts. This is to reflect not only the 'new global expansion' of the crime genre over the last few decades but also the deepening forms of social, economic, political and ecological convergence that have unfolded during this high point of globalisation (Gulddal & King, 2022, 2). This is similarly mirrored in my comparative methodological approach, which seeks to draw connections and commonalities between literary texts across temporal and geographical boundaries. As such, this Element aims to contribute towards the broader critical dismantling of the Anglo-American tradition of crime writing and criticism, placing emphasis not on the mode's various subgenres and 'subcomponents' but on the 'complexity and idiosyncrasies of the individual text' (Allan et al., 2020, 1). This includes a general movement away from considering crime fictions in the context of their distinct and separate national literary traditions, instead emphasising the global and transnational connections between works. As noted, the examination of local crime fictions, and the discussion of localism/local contexts, will still feature as part of this, but it will be situated within a broader exploration of 'extra- and transnational forces of affiliation' (King, 2021, 1249).

Such an approach is not without its problems: my own linguistic limitations and the limited availability of translated texts have unavoidably directed the selection of narratives included here. Thus, whilst this Element contains a broad representation of ecological crime fictions from across the globe – including works from Asia, Europe, Africa, South America, North America and Oceana – there is still a far greater representation of anglophone literatures on display, particularly those produced in the United States and Continental Europe. And, of course, there is also the difficult subject of specialisation, which may well be deemed essential in order to appropriately investigate the scale of works and the range of socio-political, historical, literary and cultural contexts/traditions covered here. Yet, I follow David Damrosch (2018, 21) in arguing that we need not necessarily 'face a strict either/or choice between total immersion and airy vapidity' when constructing comparative dialogues. Rather, gathering a 'full appreciation of world literature' requires us to be 'at once locally infected and translocally mobile', which will be the aim of this study (Damrosch, 2018, 21). Most significantly, my method is geared not towards the construction of a new history, tradition or subgenre of crime fiction but rather towards disrupting 'fixed cannons' by 'forging fresh connections and mutually enriching links between disparate texts and traditions', all with the aim of coming to a more complete understanding of how contemporary crime fictions are rising (or not) to the challenges posed by the global environmental crisis (Hutchinson, 2018, 4). In any case, if this Element does indeed contain limitations or oversights, as any study of this kind invariably does, it is my hope that, at the very least, it will be part of a larger conversation that pushes the study of crime fiction in new and vital directions.

1 'Continuities of Experience': Mapping the Global through the Local

Central to crime fiction's recent 'global turn' is an effort to deterritorialise critical understandings of the genre's development (and international circulation) by pushing beyond an emphasis on the traditions and conventions of national literatures. Such studies are therefore extremely useful in mapping new critical trends and identifying particular points of rupture between texts from disparate geographical locales, all the while decentring the Anglo-American 'grand narrative' that has tended to dominate critical discourse (Allan et al., 2020, 2). This 'worlding' of the genre extends to the study of ecological crime writing, where critics such as Stewart King and Marta Puxan-Oliva have similarly begun to challenge the focus on local/national contexts through the development of comparative approaches that consider ecological crime narratives beyond a single locale. Seeking to expand the terrain of crime fiction scholarship, such readings emphasise the need for new methodologies in order to better understand the mode's engagement with the scales and complexities of the climate crisis. Outside of a shared critical position, King's and Puxan-Oliva's work is united by a comparable effort to conceive of ecological crime fiction as a subgenre in its own right, one with a specific set of thematic and/or stylistic conventions. More specifically, it is ecological crime narratives that extend 'beyond the nation' – offering readers a 'broader perspective of the world' through the adaptation of their particular aesthetic forms – that are of particular interest to King and Puxan-Oliva, and constitute the predominant focus of their respective comparative approaches (King, 2021, 1240). In other words, both emphasise crime texts that have developed a sense of 'the global' *formally* through their specific narrative arrangements, and look to differentiate these examples from more 'localised' environmental crime stories where ecological considerations are either constrained by the mode's conventions or marginal to the story. Whilst they both still stress the value of the local scene, particularly in revealing the multivalent scales of the climate crisis, it is a form of localism that has value principally in its appeal to larger global dynamics.

Before considering these forms of ecological crime fiction that move between different spatial scales (which will be the focus of Section 2), it is first worth reflecting on the role of more spatially enclosed ecological crime stories – including those where ecological discourses are more latent in their thematic or formal material – in representing, and reflecting upon, the global climate crisis. Despite King's and Puxan-Olivia's emphasis on the scalar flexibility of particular forms of contemporary crime writing, one of the quirks of the genre's 'internationalisation' has been the seeming reconcentration of the local as a site of meaning. It is a point argued by Eva Erdmann (2009, 12), who goes as far as to suggest that contemporary crime fiction is very much distinguished by a focus 'not on the crime itself, but on the setting'. Slavoj Žižek (2003) makes a similar claim, arguing that the chief impact of 'globalisation' on the development of the crime novel can be observed 'in its dialectical counterpoint: the specific locale, a particular provincial environment as the story's setting'. Gulddal and King (2022) are ultimately critical of this stance, arguing that Erdmann and Žižek seem to understand 'transnational appropriation' as merely 'a matter of adding palm trees or snowy landscapes, spicing up the narrative with exotic cultural practices [but] not fundamentally altering the way the story is told' (11). Pepper and Schmid (2016, 3) are similarly dismissive, suggesting that such readings rest on the 'facile analogy between the detective [and the] tour guide ... where the sheer range of perspectives on offer ... becomes a cause for uncritical celebration'. Whilst it is certainly true that limiting the field of world crime fiction to an 'opportunity for literary tourism' reduces its critical value, there seems a more substantial argument being made by Erdmann and Žižek here, one that is perhaps oversimplified in these critical rebuttals (Gulddal & King, 2022, 11). A clue to this can be seen later in Žižek's essay:

> Today, the exception, the eccentric locale, is the rule. The global stance of 20th-century Modernism asserted itself in the guise of cosmopolitanism or membership of a global Americanised culture; this is no longer the case. A truly global citizen today is one who discovers or returns to (identifies with) particular roots, who displays a specific communal identity. The 'global order' is in the end only the frame and container of this shifting multitude of particular identity. (Žižek, 2003)

Far from reiterating a generalised observation regarding the geographical diversity of the genre, here Žižek seems to be making a rather specific point about the impact of globalisation on the contemporary crime novel's particular ideological and aesthetic shape. In other words, counter to the claim that crime fiction 'increasingly transcends, if not invalidates national boundaries', what Žižek identifies here, rather, is a heightened *intensification* of the local, an almost active drive towards reterritorialisation as a direct means of response to the forces of global capitalism (Matzke and Mühleisen, 2006, 8). To what extent, then, does this 'insistent localism' actually represent the 'true essence of globalisation' in contemporary crime narratives, rather than its diametrical opposite (Schmid, 2016, 22)? And, as such, what role can these typically 'local' ecological crime novels still play in shaping our understanding of the complexities of the global climate crisis?

Crucially, whilst it may be the responsibility of the writer (or artist) to look beyond the current 'grid of literary forms and conventions' that have come to shape the collective 'narrative imagination', it is the work of the critic to uncover 'continuities of experience' between (and across) works that might otherwise be constrained by the boundaries or discontinuities of their particular aesthetic modes (Ghosh, 2016, 7, 62). This is particularly true if, as Žižek suggests, one of the consequences of globalisation has been an increased focus on local spatial attachments within contemporary crime narratives. In this way, and notwithstanding the kinds of scalar resistance that the Anthropocene poses to literary configurations such as the (crime) novel, more typically localised or rooted textual representations of the climate crisis can contribute meaningfully to disentangling the occluded yet 'unbearably intimate' resonances that connect peoples, communities and ecosystems across 'vast gaps in time and space' (Ghosh, 2016, 63). We might look to the work being undertaken within the energy humanities for instruction here, where critics such as Graeme Macdonald (2017, 290) have argued for the development of a 'reformulated world-literary outlook' capable of interpreting the 'world reach of the carbon web'. This necessitates a move 'beyond comparative literature's traditional tension between object and method, and its restrictive orientations around language and translation'. Macdonald points to Lucia Boldrini's concept of nodal points – 'places, sites or geophysical phenomena, temporalities, or axial routes and/or processes and infrastructures' that bring different cultures into contact – as an example of this kind of restructured approach, one that can serve as a valuable 'compass of interpretation for energetic resource fictions' (Macdonald, 2017, 290).

This critical work will directly inform the first subsection ('This Has Everything to Do with Oil'), which, in juxtaposing two local and ostensibly unrelated petro-crime fictions – crime fictions that engage with the 'physical stuff' of oil in their thematic and/or formal content – seeks to scrutinise the highly uneven political and 'social-cultural' relations between the core and the peripheries of the 'petro-capitalist world system' (Duckert, 2021, 216; Fakhrkonandeh, 2022, 1786). Comparing Attica Locke's *Black Water Rising* (Locke, 2009) and Fernanda Melchor's *Hurricane Season* (Melchor, 2017), it will focus particularly on their respective representations of the Mexican Gulf, a regional geography that has been materially and unevenly transformed by the 'capital-intensive infrastructures' of the global oil economy (Morales Hernández, 2022, 17). In revealing the disaggregated spaces of oil's extraction and consumption, as well as the direct and indirect forms of violence that it enables, this section will attempt to map the criminal expressions of petroleum culture – or what I will term 'crude criminality' – across linguistic and geographical borders, interrogating what forms of 'aesthetic and environmental resistance' these texts are able to produce (Macdonald, 2017, 289). Here, crude criminality refers not only to the types of violent crime explicitly or implicitly produced by the conditions of petro-capitalism but also to its generally damaging, dispersed and highly obscured socio-economic effects.

The second subsection ('Benevolent Colonialism') will extend these critical methodologies beyond the energy humanities, interrogating the relationship between environmental justice and other extractive economies in Julie Janson's *Madukka the River Serpent* (Janson, 2022) and Thomas King's *Cold Skies* (King, 2018). Through similar explorations of indigenous water rights in the otherwise unrelated contexts of Australia and the United States, these novels reveal not only how capitalist infrastructures power the climate crisis but also how these ecological abuses are inextricably bound up with the brutal and exploitive violences committed against indigenous peoples and communities by the systems of settler colonialism. Tracking the continuities of experience that link geographically diverse communities from across the globe – while also considering how these texts challenge colonial knowledge systems through their narrative arrangements – this section shows how these localised injustices can be usefully located within the larger struggles for sovereignty, and fights against environmental racism, across the globe.

'This Has Everything to Do with Oil': Crude Criminality in *Black Water Rising* and *Hurricane Season*

Locke's *Black Water Rising* (Locke, 2009) is a particularly prodigious example of a 'local' ecological crime novel that self-reflexively engages with the materialities of petro-capitalism within its thematic and formal content. Set in Houston, Texas, in 1981, the novel traces the combustible social and economic landscape of the nascent Reagan administration, where rising oil prices, growing financial inequalities and unstable labour relations are positioned as the inevitable consequence of a new and aggressive series of neoliberal reform policies, typified, most notably, by the removal of price controls on gasoline, propane and US-produced crude oil. Locke uses this broad historical canvas to trace the complex and 'wide ranging entanglements of oil' on various levels (LeMenager, 2014, 133), revealing the ways in which, as protagonist and struggling lawyer/pseudo-detective Jay Porter later puts it, 'this oil thing touches everything' (Locke, 2009, 417). Locke is particularly preoccupied with the obscured nature of oil, how its dispersed movements and disaggregated locations of extraction, production and consumption ultimately collude to stymie forms of collective resistance. As Stephanie LeMenager (2014, 132) suggests, Jay's – and the text's – quest is to demystify the complex and corrupt manoeuvrings underlying neoliberal economic structures by bringing them 'back into public knowledge', rebuilding the democratic principles of 'civic space' in the process. Yet the denouement to the text, which sees many of the narrative's most powerful criminal agitators either frustrate or entirely escape the mechanisms of the law, reveals the limitations of traditional forms of the crime novel (and traditional forms of justice) in imagining resolutions that resist these multifaceted and far-reaching manifestations of power.

The tendrillic effects of petroleum energy are prefigured in the opening chapter of the text, when Jay surprises his pregnant wife Bernie with a birthday boat ride down the moonlit tributaries of the Buffalo Bayou. Looking out across the horizon of the swamp, Jay traces the movement of the polluted river – 'black like oil' – as it snakes through the 'underbelly' of the city, connecting 'all the way out to the Ship Channel and the Port of Houston' before eventually spilling out 'into the gulf of Mexico' (Locke, 2009, 4). Whilst ostensibly symbolising the deep-seated corruption coursing through the veins of Houston's political and economic institutions, this description of the bayou and its movements can equally be read as a material mapping of the viscous commodity flows of oil capital as it travels in and out of the city. This is fortified by the industrial sites of petroleum production that Jay sees crowding the skyline either side of the river, 'mere clusters of blinking lights and puffs of smoke, white against the swollen charcoal sky' (12). Locke is particularly interested in this relationship between petro-capitalism and the social/physical configurations of urban space, as underlined moments later when Jay hears the crack of a gunshot emanating from the direction of Fifth Ward: 'one of the roughest neighbourhoods in the city' (14). As Ryan Poll (2014, 176) suggests, Jay immediately assumes the particular typology of the crime – gang/street violence – owing to its proximity to an economically deprived and 'predominantly African American' region of the city. In this way, Locke quickly works to shape the reader's 'cognitive map' of Houston's stratified social space, underscoring the extent to which 'crime must always be contextualised by a robust geographic imagination' (Poll, 2014, 176). Yet Jay is incorrect in his suppositions, as he realises when he pulls a terrified woman – 'white and filthy' – from the violent currents of the bayou (Locke, 2009, 19). The presence of an expensively dressed white woman fleeing Fifth Ward brings the racial politics of the crime back into focus, prefiguring a central concern of the novel: 'the persistence of racial segregation decades after Jim Crow culture ostensibly ended' (Poll, 2014, 176).

The legacies of Jim Crow and the civil rights movement enter the narrative most explicitly via flashbacks to Jay's activist past, where we learn of his one-time affiliation with radical political organisations such as the SNCC and the Black Panthers. This culminated in a political rally where – before being detained as part of a COINTELPRO investigation – Jay intended to call for a 'nationwide boycott of some of the biggest corporations in America', particularly petrochemical companies like 'Shell and Gulf Oil' that were 'continuing to benefit from a history of colonial and economic oppression of brown people' (Locke, 2009, 265). Jay's subsequent arrest and narrow escape from incarceration signal the symbolic end of 'counterculture radicalism' in the United States, and come to define his present-day struggles to escape the country's burdened racial history by conforming to a brand of middle-class, bourgeois respectability (LeMenager, 2014, 132). Yet these inequalities continue to subsist in the stratified social arrangements that surround him, as typified by the racial tensions underscoring the fraught labour relations between the city's striking stevedores. In one section, Jay describes money as 'the new Jim Crow' and nowhere is this more evident than in the permeating influence of petro-capitalism on the fraught political, economic and urban landscapes that the text reveals (Locke, 2009, 75).

In Houston, 'the fastest growing city in the country', the text locates a potent geographical symbol of the rapid transformation of American life by the various manifestations of oil culture (Locke, 2009, 36). Locke's narrator notes how Houston has a 'curious habit of razing its own history', a point emphasised by the steel and glass high-rises – including the headquarters for Cole Oil – that now dominate the crowded downtown skyline, physically dwarfing other monuments of the city's past, like the 'squat limestone building' of city hall. As Poll (2014, 191) suggests, what Locke sketches here is the emergence of a new 'geographic history and symbolism', where 'oil capitalism has now eclipsed the power of the state'. The extent to which oil shapes the social and physical topographies of Houston is persistently underscored by Locke as the narrative progresses. We see this not only in the text's various references to 'specific sites of the oil economy' – the Cole Oil refineries, the Houston Shipping Yard – but also in its 'scenic descriptions' of a more imbricated set of 'petroleum infrastructures', such as highways, gas stops and roadside eateries

(LeMenager, 2014, 133). Much like his hard-boiled antecedents, Jay's investigative capacities are contingent on his automotive movement through the urban circuitry of the modern metropolis. Locke is hyperaware of her pseudo-detective's deep imbrication in this crude oil commodity chain, as underscored by various scenes that depict Jay paying for gasoline at the pump, where his increasing financial precarity is articulated through the prism of rising fuel prices. In the process, Jay and his perambulations around the city come to reveal the highly uneven social geographies that oil capital – and neoliberal energy markets – conspire to produce. This is indicated by the stark inequalities of Houston, which, despite its financial prosperity, is barely 'able to keep up with its own growth' (Locke, 2009, 36). Locke reveals a city 'bursting at the seams' with trash and waste, its municipal infrastructures unable to cope with the 'new businesses and housing developments going up every week' (37). This creates a parallel waste disposal market, where more affluent neighbourhoods pay private companies 'to haul their shit away', leaving streets like Jay's – lined with 'cheap rentals and shotgun houses' – entirely at 'the mercy of the city' (37). Whilst oil purports to enable a 'dynamic geography and population', Locke shows that such mobility is far from 'evenly distributed', particularly along the axes of race, gender and class (Poll, 2014, 192).

The local injustices produced by the systemic asymmetries of oil capitalism are brought into focus at the climax of the text, as Jay connects the parallel plots of murder and union unrest to the felonious machinations of the city's largest petrochemical company. It transpires that Cole Oil has been exploiting the newly deregulated oil market to hoard mass reserves of crude in abandoned salt caverns around Texas, thus manipulating the price of petroleum at the pump. This literally bubbles to the surface when Jay discovers that crude deposits have been seeping through the foundations of a town above the salt mines. After being shown the extent of the seepage by the town's one remaining resident – the obstinate Erman Ainsley – Jay reaches down to touch the crude, rolling it around his fingers like 'melted gelatine' and feeling the way it 'coats his skin completely, covering his pores, clinging like a parasite that has found an unsuspecting host' (Locke, 2009, 318). The language used here projects something agentively pernicious onto oil's viscous materiality, as Jay is unable to separate the unctuousness of the organic substance, its literal stickiness, from its pervasive commodity uses and effects. Yet what the text is really pointing to here is the kind of criminality that oil – in its commodity form – engenders, a crude criminality that clings to everything and everyone. As such, the various forms of violence and injustice that Jay encounters can all be connected to the same root cause. As the city's port commissioner puts it earlier in the novel: 'This has everything to do with oil' (79).

Whereas *Black Water Rising* is explicit in its interrogation of the social, economic and ecological impacts of petroleum culture, grounding its plot in a key moment (and place) in the global history of oil modernity, Melchor's *Hurricane Season* (Melchor, 2017) offers a subtler examination of these same effects, tracing their more occluded materialisations in the 'abject corners of extractive economies' (González, 2020). Despite therefore providing very different 'novelistic registrations of oil frontiers', together these texts construct a revealing imaginative map of the vast and highly uneven territories that bound the Gulf of Mexico, a region that, since the 1970s, has been markedly and disproportionately shaped by the dictates and infrastructures of the global oil industry (Macdonald, 2017, 289). As such, the gulf has become 'a forceful signifier' not only of the inequalities and 'contradictions' produced by petro-capitalism but also of the 'deep nexus between accumulation and the criminal realms hidden behind the zones of enclosure and transnational corporate rule' (Morales Hernández, 2022, 17–22). *Hurricane Season* grounds these fraught social and economic relations in the fictional town of La Matosa, a marginalised and deprived rural community located in the coastal state of Veracruz, some 700 miles south of Galveston Bay. The narrative ostensibly centres on the brutal murder of a local transwoman known as 'The Witch', whose rotting corpse is discovered dumped in an irrigation canal in the opening pages of the text. The Witch is notorious within the community for providing free abortions for sex workers and for hosting drug-fuelled sex parties where troops of local men come to fulfil their sordid sexual fantasies. Rumour and superstition encircle the Witch, with many believing – amongst other supernatural speculations – that she is in possession of a secret fortune stashed somewhere within the hollows of her decrepit mansion. Loved and despised in equal measure, she becomes a canvas upon which the community projects its deepest fears and desires, as well as a lightning rod for its repressed rage and simmering violence.

The novel is by no means a 'whodunit' in the traditional sense, as the guilty parties are revealed soon after the body is discovered. Instead, the circumstances that precipitated the Witch's death are revealed incrementally across eight single-paragraph chapters, all narrated from the coalescing perspectives of several individuals from within the community. The febrile social relations of La Matosa become mirrored in the text's frenzied, vulgar and highly digressive narrative style, where sentences run breathlessly across several pages and shift disorientingly between a diverse assemblage of voices and temporal markers. The result is a feverish swirl of erratic and highly unreliable narration, as Melchor draws deeply on the language of gossip, rumour and superstition to reveal a community blinded and immobilised by its own destructive mythologies. As such, the murder of the Witch becomes a prism through which Melchor examines the broader economic forces and political inequalities that have shaped, and continue to shape, modern La Matosa. Alongside the stark manifestations of homophobia, misogyny and sexual violence that the text reveals, it also provides several fractured references to the town's turbulent recent history, beginning with the hurricane-triggered landslide of 1978, which saw the majority of the town and its residents buried under a 'tumult of rocks' (Melchor, 2017, 26). Although La Matosa was rebuilt in the aftermath – 'dotted once more with shacks and shanties raised on the bones of [the dead]' – it was the discovery of oil deposits north of the town that precipitated the rapid reshaping of its material and economic geographies, beginning with the construction of a giant superhighway connecting the 'port and the capital' to the newly found wells (Melchor, 2017, 28). Soon repopulated by outsiders 'lured by the trail of banknotes that the oil trucks left in their wake' (Melchor, 2017, 28), the town developed by creating a 'buoyant but precarious parallel market' of cantinas, hotels and food stalls, all geared towards servicing the traffic of engineers and labourers shuttling back and forth from the adjacent oil fields (González, 2020). Yet, despite their promises of prosperity, these extractive infrastructures only bring further pain and suffering, with the town steadily falling 'victim to neoliberal austerity policies, economic crisis, and the rise of the drug trade' (González, 2020). What is left behind is a sparse and crumbling landscape of brothels, strip clubs and bars, and a populace ravaged by violence, disease, economic insecurity and energy poverty.

The oil company creates an economic stranglehold on the local community, with many of the residents seeing the highly coveted (and unionised) jobs at the wells as their only means of escape from the day-to-day struggles of life in La Matosa. This is typified by Luismi (the murderer of the Witch), who believes that he is destined for a technician's job, having been promised one by his former lover, an engineer at the company. Yet Luismi's stepfather, Munra, knows that this is a 'goddam pipe dream', as the company – one organised around private economic interests and nepotistic hierarchal structures – has 'never hired anyone who wasn't an immediate relative or recommended by those at the top' (Melchor, 2017, 77). Luismi's emotional investment in the benevolence of the oil company is both misguided and heavily ironic, indicating a broader obliviousness within the community towards the root causes of their own subjugation. As Barbara Halla (2020) suggests, the residents of La Matosa are unable to perceive the deeply imbricated relationship between their material hardships and these larger economic forces. Instead, they place blame on more ephemeral influences, be they the Witch's satanic spells or the malignant atmospheric pressures produced by heatwaves and storms. This sense of abstraction is similarly evident in the aesthetic arrangements of the text itself, where the discordant fluctuations between perspectives and temporalities reflect the violent obscuration of cause and effect under neoliberalism. In the process, Melchor examines how these occluded extractive spaces, or 'sacrifice zones', allow for the proliferation of certain forms of violence, particularly those that are commensurate to the sustainment of the economic system itself (Lerner, 2010, 2). Although Steve Lerner principally uses 'sacrifice zone' to refer to frontline communities that have been disproportionately exposed to toxic or hazardous chemicals by state or capitalist enterprises, the term has also become increasingly associated with the 'economic and political violence of extractavism', particularly in the context of Latin America (Bolados García, 2023). In this sense, *Hurricane Season* reflects upon what James A. Tyner (2016, 10) terms 'the market logics of letting die', that is, the strategic disavowal and abandonment of lives – through the enforcement of political, social and economic practice – that are deemed without utility or that otherwise 'fail to conform to the dictates of capital accumulation'. As such, it becomes possible to read the brutal murder of the Witch and the other instances of unfathomable violence that the text discloses as the 'inchoate symptom of an underlying socioeconomic condition', one that the residents of La Matosa can neither perceive nor understand (Pepper, 2016, 234).

Although offering seemingly dissimilar and unconnected examinations of 'oil's frontierism', *Hurricane Season* and *Black Water Rising* share certain 'cultural affinities and world-ecological connections' rooted in the 'unifying resource systems of petrocapitalism' (Macdonald, 2017, 300). More specifically, they trace a compelling regional history of the second oil regime, revealing how, since the energy crisis of 1973, the communities and geographies that comprise the Gulf of Mexico have been dramatically and disproportionately shaped by oil modernity's pervasive infrastructures and uneven commodity flows. In this sense, *Hurricane Season* can be positioned as a kind of spiritual sequel to *Black Water Rising* in that it obliquely reveals the detrimental consequences of the economic reform policies instituted in the early years of the Reagan administration. In the process, both novels work to demystify the forms of 'crude criminality' that oil culture engenders, underscoring not only the implicit and explicit relationships between petro-capitalism and violent crimes (murder, sexual violence, etc.) but also the more general permeation of oil in the workings of everyday life, where individuals are inculcated (often unknowingly) into forms of criminal complicity that disrupt clear boundaries between perpetrator and victim. Yet both texts ultimately struggle to offer forms of resistance to these highly dispersed dynamics from within the aesthetic and thematic bounds of the typically 'territorialised' crime novel, revealing the need for new modes of expression that move beyond the realms of the nation-state.

Despite *Black Water Rising*'s 'depictions of strike/labour conditions and worker unrest', these protests soon collapse under political and economic pressure. Moreover, whilst Jay intends to file a civil suit against Cole Oil for property encroachment, there is little sense that this is a fight he can realistically win. *Hurricane Season*, meanwhile, ends with another impending storm threatening La Matosa, an elemental force that the residents blame for a new spate of violent crimes ravaging the town: 'crimes of passion, as the journalists call them' (Melchor, 2017, 220). Still unable to perceive the real cause of their plight, neither they (nor we) are left with any 'hope that the situation will ever be any different' (Pepper, 2016, 234).

'Benevolent Colonialism': Capitalism, Colonialism and Environmental Justice in *Madukka the River Serpent* and *Cold Skies*

The previous section looked to establish continuities of experience between two local and unconnected petrocrime fictions, tracing the criminal materialisations of petrocapitalism at the core and periphery of the world carbon economy. The next section will continue this examination of the relationship between crime and extractive economies, juxtaposing two recent indigenous crime fictions from Australia and the United States. Through their analogous examinations of Indigenous water rights, these texts underscore the extent to which 'environmental justice must be placed at the centre of considerations of the Anthropocene, framing the latter as not just a geophysical concept but a biopolitical one' (Manning, 2024, 34). In the process, they expose the 'inextricable links between settler colonialism and the violence of climate crisis in the anthropocene era', making visible the legacies and continuations of harm that have defined, and continue to define, the relationship between land, race and power in both the United States and Australia (Tillett, 2024, 282). Nonetheless, this section will again question what forms of aesthetic resistance these texts are capable of producing, particularly from within the territorially and temporally confined structures of the 'local' crime novel.

Indigenous Australian playwright Julie Janson's recent eco-crime novel *Madukka the River Serpent* is, in many ways, characteristic of a broader category of contemporary Australian crime fiction where the relationship between land and violence takes centre stage. Rachel Fetherston points to texts like Jane Harper's *The Dry* (Harper, 2016), Greg Mclean's *Wolf Creek* (Mclean, 2014) and Garry Disher's *Bitter Wash Road* (Disher, 2013) as indicative in this regard, all of which connect the 'terror of the outback' with a deeper (and often implicit) set of political and environmental anxieties (Fetherson, 2023, 78). Yet Janson – a *Burruberongal*

woman of Darug Nation ancestry – moves beyond these more ambient examinations of place making and belonging, instead providing an unambiguous look at
the relationship between the 'criminal violences' of settler colonialism – both
historical and recurring – and the 'equally entrenched' and wholly related 'criminal violences' wrought against the environment as a result of these very same
systems (Tillett, 2023, 282). The novel takes place in 2020 and is set in the rural
town of Wilga, northern New South Wales, a fictional community situated
somewhere along the Darling River. As Stewart King suggests, Wilga is by no
means an 'idyllic country town' (King, 2023, n.p.), as emphasised in Janson's
opening description of its dusty desert landscapes, 'ash-filled streets', 'iron mesh'–
covered storefronts and 'stinking green river of dead fish' (Janson, 2022, n.p.). For
the omniscient narrator, this 'dusty desolation' is not only a stark reminder of how
'outback towns were shrivelling up' but also a recursive symptom of what they
term 'benevolent colonialism'. As indicated by her first novel, *Benevolence*,
Janson is particularly interested in the discourse of 'good intentions' and how
this has 'propped up' many of the 'foundational myths of Australia since colonisation' (Kavanagh, 2020). Through the economic and ecological depravation of
Wilga, Janson thus continues her political excavation of what Bec Kavanagh
(2020) calls 'the realities of kindness', revealing 'the damage, the arrogance, the
violence that have been buried beneath the term'.

The protagonist of Janson's novel is Aunty June, a 'fifty-year-old' aboriginal
'beauty . . . born of the clay plains, dust and kangaroo' (Janson, 2022, n.p.). As
the novel opens, June has just completed a 'TAFE course in investigative
services', a thirty-hour online training program that qualifies her to operate as
a private detective, '[just] like she had seen on a TV show . . . [a] brave woman
fighting for justice' (Janson, 2022, n.p.). June's first case, and the text's primary
mystery, centres on the disappearance of 'cousin Thommo', a Murri activist and
'ecological hero' with links to a radical environmentalist group. When the local
police – led by the racist Sargent Blackett – refuse to treat Thommo's disappearance as suspicious, June takes the investigation into her own hands. This
missing person's case becomes the conduit through which Janson explores
a larger environmental conspiracy threatening to destroy the town, one that
connects the rapid disappearance of the Darling River – a waterway already
damaged by climate change – to the pernicious extractive practices of the cotton
industry. The siphoning off of water by 'big irrigators' threatens not only to
destroy the local community and its surrounding ecosystems – including the
mass extinction of animal and plant life – but also to erase many indigenous
'cultures and traditions that are deeply tied to the river system' (Fetherston,
2023, 87). For June and the wider community, the Darling River operates as an
important 'dreaming track', a 'winding path' of imagination, tradition and

storied memory that connects 'like a spider web to every living thing', keeping culture and 'hope alive' (Janson, 2022, n.p.). The drying out of the dreaming track, and the attendant extinction of sacred totems such as the Murray Cod, is therefore a 'genocide' to the spirit of the community. As one local Elder puts it: '[If] the totems die, then we die. How do we live when the animals become extinct?' (Janson, 2022, n.p.). The use of the word 'genocide' is significant here and points to the destruction of the river not only as an ecological crime but as a recursive expression of a more embedded form of colonial violence. Crucially, what Janson points to here is the way in which indigenous communities 'often understand their vulnerability to climate change as an intensification of coloni-ally induced environmental changes' (Whyte, 2017, 154). In other words, anthropogenic climate change is experienced as both an extension and a concentration of the ideologies and practices that, under colonialism, allowed for the violent erasure of peoples and lands in the endless pursuit of profit. June's brother William makes this connection explicitly later in the text, describing the community's ongoing struggles with the impacts of capitalism as 'invasion and conquering all over again' (Janson, 2022, n.p.).

In the case of the disappearing Darling River, this violence is as much epistemic as it is ecological, and comes to signify the broader (and ongoing) effacement of indigenous cultures, narratives and histories. Janson is particu-larly interested in the relationship between memory and landscape, and, at several points, takes us back to buried moments in Australia's violent colonial history. Early in the text, we learn that June's family live adjacent to a spot 'where terrible murders had taken place, the soil full of human fragments, skin, and hair and terror and murder' (Janson, 2022, n.p.). Although there are no material traces or monuments that speak to, or commemorate, these atrocities, June can feel their traumatic resonances 'oozing from the grey earth' like a 'river [of] blood coming from below', a kind of 'stinking trickle, a miasma' that 'would never go away' (Janson, 2022, n.p.). The palimpsestic land speaks a brutal counter history of modern Australia, challenging the stories of 'valiant English explorers and white pioneering spirit' by exposing the death and destruction upon which these myths were built (Janson, 2022, n.p.). Ghosts and hauntings become central to the text's construction of an alternate know-ledge system, one that counters the epistemologies, ontologies and discourses that served to legitimise the violent and discriminatory practices of colonial rule. This is typified by Aunty June's methods of detection, which 'unravel and disrupt' these 'epistemic sites of hierarchized power' through the strategic destabilisation of 'dichotomous categorisations' such as '"primitive/civilized", "rational/irrational" and "traditional-modern"' (Sharma, 2021, 25). As well as following material clues to Thommo's disappearance – much like in the

Western tradition of detective fiction – Aunt June is frequently directed by hauntings and materialisations from the spirit world. These 'goonges' not only actualise the otherwise invisible continuum of cruelties perpetrated against indigenous communities but also emphasise a deep 'cultural and spiritual connection to place', unsettling the 'notion of *terra nullius*' (Fetherston, 2023, 88). It is in this way that Janson moves the frame of the novel beyond Thommo's death, as June's investigation unravels a host of interlocking crimes – including political corruption, corporate maleficence, sexual violence, land dispossession, resource extraction, police violence and racism – that connect the injustices of the present to the injustices of the past. As June says when speaking of Thommo's death: 'It isn't about one person. It's about much more, who we are' (Janson, 2022, n.p.).

In the same way that Janson presents other ways of 'knowing and construct-ing meaning about the world' through June's methods of detection, she offers a similarly reconstituted understanding of truth and justice through the text's highly spectral denouement, one that counters and disrupts the hegemonic (and discriminatory) mechanisms of the state (Dhillon, 2022, 3). As Fetherston (2023, 87) suggests, a significant part of the novel's reclaiming of native identities comes from 'undermining' the 'coloniser's legal systems and processes' – and its cultural vehicles, such as the detective novel – through the use of 'indigenous cultural knowledge'. This is indicated not only by Steve Allunga – an ecological protester killed in police custody – whose 'goonge' proceeds to haunt the officers responsible for his death but also by Madukka the water serpent, a spiritual manifestation of the Darling River, which, at the climax of the text, enacts retribution against the corrupt Sargent Blackett by dragging him under water during a violent storm, 'drown[ing] him in its rage and tumult' (Janson, 2022, n.p.). The serpent functions as a form of political and ecological restitution, providing justice for those harmed (and erased) by the violence of the settler-colonial state, and returning clean flood water, 'luscious and fast flowing' (Janson, 2022, n.p.), to the landscapes otherwise ravaged by the economic primacies of these same power structures. This forms part of a series of ostensible 'resolutions' at the novel's end, including the solving of Thommo's murder, which June connects to a violent local 'bikie' called Bam Bam. Yet Janson is also wary of neat endings, with the text's closing pages underscoring the broader limitations of the crime genre – particularly its more 'traditional generic forms' – to provide 'justice for the systemic violence experienced by Indigenous peoples' (Pepper & Schmid, 2016, 16; see also King, 2023). The replacement of Brackett and Johnson with 'two new police officers' is indicative in this regard, suggesting a continuation, rather than a disruption, of what came before. This extends to the larger plot of resource extraction and to the forms of environmental discrimination that it permits. It is telling that, in the final pages, June and her family take the decision to leave Wilga for good, underscoring the ongoing displacement of indigenous peoples and communities in Australia.

Though praising *Madukka*'s excavation of the buried histories of Australia's First Nations people, Stewart King (2023) suggests that the novel is less successful in fostering a 'shared sense of community central to addressing the environmental catastrophe that affects us all'. Given King's previous work on ecological crime fiction, what he is pointing to are the limitations of eco-localism (or reterritorialisation) as a means of political/artistic resistance to global environmental crises. More specifically, he is suggesting that there are certain aesthetic constraints that prohibit the novel's capacity to cultivate a more encompassing planetary vision. Here King follows the work of Ursula K. Heise, who advocates for an eco-cosmopolitan approach to environmentalism that is premised no longer 'on ties to local places but on ties to territories and systems [that] encompass the planet as a whole' (Heise, 2008, 10). For King (2021), as with Heise, this necessitates the cultivation of new forms and narrative strategies capable of moving beyond the typically delimited temporal and spatial scope of the (crime) novel. Whilst it is true that Janson's text is largely circumscribed by the local scene – and thus symptomatic of the formal limitations of 'local' ecological crime fictions – this 'sense of planet' can be cultivated critically, I suggest, by tracing the commonalities and continuities of experience that connect ostensibly disparate local communities, and their respective struggles for sovereignty, from across the globe. It is in this way that Thomas King's *Cold Skies* (King, 2018), another localised ecological crime novel, can be brought into useful dialogue with Janson's work, highlighting how the economic primacies of global capitalism, and its attendant ecological effects, manifest in comparable ways throughout the world. As such, local struggles for environmental justice can be positioned and understood within the context of larger global systems.

Cold Skies is the third in Thomas King's series of six crime novels featuring Cherokee detective Thumps DreadfulWater, and, like *Madukka the River Serpent*, it similarly examines the relationship between the 'criminal violences of capitalist driven settler colonialism' and those of the 'profit-driven climate crisis' (Tillett, 2023, 283). The text's primary mystery centres on the co-owners of an engineering company called Orion Technologies, both of whom turn up murdered on the eve of a major water conference set to take place in the small town of Chinook. The pair had been due to share the results of a 'revolutionary' new technology designed to measure and map aquifers, one that could potentially 'change the face' of water conservation and groundwater management. Perhaps more significantly, this same technology could also theoretically be deployed to survey oil and

gas deposits, which, as Thumps' friend Archie notes, would have seismic consequences for the energy resource industry: 'The last thing extraction companies
want is a method that accurately measure reserves . . . it could be the end of their
empires' (King, 2018, 129). The plot is further complicated by the location of the
aquifer, a large section of which runs directly beneath the Blackfoot reservation. It
transpires that, two years prior, Orion Technologies had negotiated a ten-year
lease with the state to install monitoring wells along the Bear Hump, a section of
tribal land previously demarcated as reservation territory. The Blackfoot chief,
Claire Merchant, subsequently tried to file an injunction, only to find that the
original 1836 land treaty had been 'unilaterally changed' by the US Senate
without their knowledge. 'There's a strong oral record of exactly what we
agreed', Claire tells Thumps, 'but every time we go to court, oral testimony has
been ruled unreliable' (King, 2018, 205).

Here we again see 'the intertwined processes of settler colonialism and
resource extraction', where the sustainment of rapacious capitalist infrastructures
is contingent on the ongoing exploitation of indigenous lands and peoples
(Follett, 2023, 382). Like Janson, King situates these present-day violences as
a continuation of the historic atrocities inflicted upon native communities under
the auspices of white colonial power, as he similarly looks to excavate the brutal
and long-buried truths underpinning frontier mythologies. These repressed traumas are brought to the surface moments after Thumps learns of the alterations to
the 1836 treaty, when the omniscient narrator takes us back to the Removal Act of
1830, which 'allowed the government to strip the tribes along the eastern
seaboard of their land' (King, 2018, 205). This laid the groundwork for the US
army to 'invade Cherokee territory' eight years later, forcing 'thirteen thousand
people into concentration camps' before marching them west to Indian Territory
(205). 'More than four thousand Cherokee died on the two-thousand-mile trek',
the narrator tells us, 'two deaths for every mile' (205). As with Janson, these
surfacings (or hauntings) become constitutive to King's construction of
a knowledge system that challenges the dominant discourses of coloniality.
Thus, notwithstanding its ostensibly 'formulaic' appeals to the conventions and
traditions of genre, it is in this way that King's detective fiction cultivates a form
of aesthetic resistance to the deeply tangled structures of settler colonialism and
anthropogenic climate change, one that Pascale Manning similarly identifies in
King's 'literary' fiction (Follett, 2023, 383). Focusing on two other of Thomas
King's novels, *Green Grass, Running Water* (King, 1993) and *Truth and Bright
Water* (King, 1999), Manning (2024, 35) argues that, through their content and
style, these texts acknowledge 'states of dislocation, historical entanglement, and
socio-material interconnection as the condition of reality in our catastrophic
present', thereby inculcating readers into ways of thinking that recognise 'the

indivisibility of the projects of decolonization and environmental justice'. For Manning, it is by 'contextualising the realities' of the present in this way – and situating readers in 'narrative environments that reveal the interlinking forces conspiring to generate the climate crisis' – that King is able to cultivate a form of 'anthropocene realism' (Manning, 2024, 24) capable of contending with what Amitav Ghosh (2016, 63) describes as 'forces of unimaginable magnitude'.

Whilst perhaps more formally constrained than the texts cited by Manning – owing, in large part, to its mostly orthodox adherence to the narrative expect-ations of the police procedural – *Cold Skies* still continues this work to some degree, revealing how 'indigenous subject positions' must 'variously negotiate' the 'ongoing hazards of empire' (Manning, 2024, 34). As part of this, King interrogates the assumptions and stereotypes underlying many Euro-American conceptualisations of indigenous environmentalism, particularly the critical tendency to position indigenous peoples as 'environmentalists par excellence' (Nadasdy, 2005, 292). This is typified in an early section of the text, when Thumps visits the Blackfoot reservation with his friend Moses and Moses' grandson, Cooley:

> "There was an anthropologist who came by and told Moses that Indians were
> in tune with nature. Said that Indians could feel the rhythms of the earth."
> Moses stretched his legs and wiggled his toes into the short prairie grass.
> "What about it, grandson, you feel the rhythms?"
> "Nope," said Cooley, "what about you?"
> "Nope," said Moses (King, 2018, 81).

Here King alludes to a common stereotype, one rooted in the assumption that 'indigenous people live in perfect harmony' with the natural world and should therefore serve as an 'inspiration for those in industrial society who seek a new, more sustainable relationship with the environment' (Nadasdy, 2005, 292). For King, this outside co-option – or indeed production – of indigenous cultural knowledge is colonial power manifested in a different guise and thus works only to further substantiate pre-existing inequalities and injustices. As Paul Nadasdy (2005, 293) suggests, not only does this perception of ecological nobility deny the reality of native people's lives, thus reducing the 'rich diversity of their beliefs, values, social relations, and practices to a one-dimensional caricature', but it also imposes impossibly high standards that are incapable of being met. These tensions factor directly into the text's ambivalent denouement, where Thumps discovers that the corporate interest in the Bear Hump actually stems from its rich deposits of red beryl. This ends with Claire Merchant negotiating a deal with rabid capitalist Randall Boomper Austin, one that will see the community financially remunerated for the mining of its lands. As Alec Follett

(2023, 384) suggests, on the one hand this can be read as a 'hopeful' conclusion, with Merchant's deal 'standing in contrast' to the many times that indigenous communities have been forcefully dispossessed by extractive projects and fraudulent land claims. However, it also means that the novel is able to resolve its criminal plot only 'within a settler-colonial framework, where Merchant's options are limited' to the extraction of beryl either 'for a fee or for free' (Follett, 2023, 384). As with Janson's text, we are left with an uncomfortable sense of subsistence, the feeling that nothing has materially changed despite the text's ostensible challenging of the conventions and knowledge systems most frequently aligned with the realist (and local) crime novel. The result is a somewhat orthodox denouement, one that awkwardly attempts to reconcile the complex environmental injustices it reveals (both past and present) with the crime novel's normative drive for closure. Individually, then, both *Madukka* and *Cold Skies* are ultimately constrained by their appeal to a particular set of aesthetic parameters, limiting the forms of resistance that they are able to produce from within. Comparatively, however, they reveal a detailed picture of the systems and structures that connect many disparate and subjugated communities around the world, underscoring the important role that local fictions can still play in revealing, and demystifying, the small-scale and often occluded manifestations of larger global injustices.

2 The 'Glocal' Turn: Ecological Crime Fiction and the Re/Deterritorialised State

Whilst Section 1 pointed to a methodology for constructing 'continuities of experience' between ostensibly unconnected and locally situated texts, it told us very little about how, and to what extent, ecological crime narratives are pushing their own aesthetic boundaries in ways that reframe 'localism from a globalist environmental perspective' (Heise, 2008, 9). It is a question that can be contextualised within a broader contemporary debate regarding the capacity of our existing literary and cultural forms to meet the material and representational challenges posed by the climate crisis. Ghosh (2016, 61) has drawn specific attention to the 'delimited horizon' of the novel, a mode which, he argues, is able to 'conjure up worlds that become real precisely because of their finitude and distinctiveness'. For Ghosh (2016, 62), the novel is characterised by certain spatial and temporal 'discontinuities', making the contrastingly 'insistent, inescapable continuities' of the Anthropocene fundamentally incompatible with the techniques and conventions most closely associated with the form. Timothy Clark (2015, 13) similarly acknowledges the representational challenge that the 'unreadability' of the Anthropocene poses to our existing creative and critical modes, as it demands that we think in scales of space and time that significantly alter 'the way that many once familiar issues appear'. As such, Clark (2015, 24) questions whether the demands of the anthropocene can be met 'by new forms of artistic and cultural innovation or, more darkly, [if] certain limits of the human imagination, artistic representation and the capacity of understanding [are] now being reached'.

It is a query that has particular ramifications for our reading of crime fiction, especially if we are to follow Ghosh's contention that the role of novelistic setting is primarily to function as a 'vessel for the exploration of the ultimate instance of discontinuity: the nation state' (Ghosh, 2016, 59). Here Ghosh alludes to Benedict Anderson's work in *Imagined Communities*, in which Anderson (2006, 25) attributes the emergence of the nation as a form of 'imagined community' to the rise of print capitalism, particularly the proliferation of 'two forms of imagining which first flowered in Europe in the eighteenth century: the novel and newspaper'. Presenting readers with newly situated configurations of time and space, as well as a previously inconceivable sense of connectivity between individuals and events, these forms provided 'the technical means' for representing 'the kind of imagined community that is the nation' (Anderson, 2006, 25). Whilst Anderson is largely preoccupied with the provenance and workings of the realist novel, this association between popular narrative forms and nationhood can be usefully extended to the emergence of crime fiction. With its strong attachments to place, the crime novel is, perhaps more than any other literary mode, 'especially suited to the task of imagining nationhood', as it is fundamentally concerned with questions of 'community and transgression' (King, 2011, 52). For Pepper (2016, 1), these preoccupations are rooted in the knotted relationship between the development of the genre and the establishment 'of the modern bureaucratic state', which he traces back to narratives and discourses on crime, law and order circulating in Paris and London in the early eighteenth century. Whereas the state often remains oblique in other literary forms, Pepper (2016, 1) suggests that, from inception, crime stories have routinely thematised and made visible the 'institutional bodies, policing practices, legal processes and judicial norms that make up the criminal justice system', giving 'tangible shape' to the state's 'labyrinthine' machinations and institutional arrangements. In this sense, the crime novel has played – and continues to play – an important yet largely overlooked role in the production of place-based national identities. As Stephen Rachman (2010, 20) argues: 'If the urban newspaper helped to constitute "imagined communities" of the nineteenth century ... then the detective tale was a second-order operation within that community, a viral form in which readers recognized a new fictive expression of a modern social order.'

The point here is that crime narratives present the most concentrated expression of this deep interrelationship between the novel and the nation-state. The highly dispersed and transnational nature of the Anthropocene therefore poses an arguably greater challenge to the mode precisely because of its characteristically constrained temporal and territorial reach. How capable is the crime novel, then, of interrogating the dense enmeshments and variable scales of this new and highly contingent global terrain? Or, as Pepper and Schmid (2016) put it: '[H]ow well is it able [to] think beyond the state?' (7). This is a key question that has preoccupied several scholars seeking to move the study of ecological (and world) crime fiction away from local or place-based considerations. Stewart King (2021), in particular, has sought to theorise a new mode of ecological crime novel, one that is more narratively adept at moving beyond the customarily demarcated jurisdiction of the state. King points to *L'olor de la pluja* (*The Smell of Rain*, 2006) by the Catalan novelist Jordi de Manuel (2006) and *Parantaja* (*The Healer*, [2010] 2014) by Finnish author Antti Tuomainen ([2010] 2014) as key examples of 'crimate fictions', texts that 'both narrate the climate catastrophe through the popular conventions of the crime genre and apply the genre's central ideological concerns with culpability and criminality to the climate crisis' (King, 2021, 1237). For King, what makes such texts unique – outside of their thematisations of environmental criminality – is their ability to move between 'the specific space of crime, its investigation and the larger world' (1237). Through their scalar flexibility, such texts allow us to 'identify and appreciate local concerns as well as developing extra- and transnational forces of affiliation on which the eco-cosmopolitanism that is needed to address the contemporary environmental challenge is based' (1249). Here King explicitly aligns his work with a broader international or global turn in contemporary ecocritical thought, one characterised by a pointed movement away from a critical investment in environmentally based localisms. As such, he seeks to follow the work of Heise and Buell in exploring what 'new possibilities for ecological awareness' inhere in forms of crime fiction that are 'increasingly detached from their anchorings in particular geographies' (Heise, 2008, 13).

The tension between the local and the global forms the basic framework for this section, which will examine ecological crime narratives that move between interconnected spatial scales in a style approximating King's 'crimate fictions'. Whilst acknowledging that these 'glocal' texts – texts characterised by an explicit emphasis on both local and global considerations – do succeed, in some capacity, in elucidating or demystifying the complex and multifaceted connections between local crimes and larger global forces, I will suggest that they tend to offer ambivalent, even contradictory, responses to the networked dynamics that they reveal, forestalling, in either case, the kind of eco-cosmopolitan awareness that King attributes to them. The first subsection ('Local Crimes from Global Seeds') will focus on *Pale Horses* by South African writer Jassy MacKenzie (2012) and *Don't Cry Tai Lake* by Chinese American author Qiu Xiaolong (2012), arguing that both texts express a reignited faith in the sovereignty of the state in the face of globally orientated eco-capitalist threats or conspiracies. This drive towards reterritorialisation, one that seems to position national bureaucratic structures as central to maintaining social cohesion in the face of global environmental challenges, is intimately bound up with the crime genre's normative drive towards resolution, meaning that such texts end up resisting, rather than affirming, a kind of planetary consciousness.

The second subsection ('Broken Borders and Climate Dystopias') will examine two texts that move in the counter direction, exposing the increasing powerlessness and irrelevancy of the state in the face of extralegal environmental crimes and impending global cataclysms. Focusing on Tuomainen's *The Healer* (Tuomainen, [2010] 2014) and *Earthly Remains* by American novelist Donna Leon (2017), it will ultimately question the capacity of such texts to envision 'less territorially defined forms of inhabitation', arguing that the deterritorialised spaces that they reveal tend to possess violent and confounding – rather than cosmopolitan and revelatory – dimensions (Heise, 2008, 207). To say then, as Stewart King does, that these texts 'educate readers to act ethically' (King, 2021, 1247) – and to modify their own behaviours in the present – implies that their ethical arguments are necessarily clear-cut, which, in the examples discussed here, is far from the case. What tends to characterise these texts, rather, is a kind of critical inertia, one that becomes closely associated with expressions of pessimism, powerlessness and guilt. Taken together, these two subsections suggest that glocal environmental crime fictions are still largely constrained by their adherence to traditional genre forms and conventions. The result is a somewhat immobilising push and pull between two competing visions of state sovereignty, neither of which is entirely successful in articulating a global ecological understanding or in expressing hope for a changed planet. Nevertheless – and anticipating the focus of Section 3 – what we can begin to see here are the ways in which contemporary ecological crime narratives are striving to forge new 'aesthetic templates' for conveying 'a dual vision of earth as a whole and of the different earths that are shaped by varying cultural contexts' (Heise, 2008, 210).

Local Crimes from Global Seeds: Environmental Crime and the Reterritorialised State in *Pale Horses* and *Don't Cry Tai Lake*

Jassy Mackenzie's Johannesburg-based crime novels featuring private investigator Jade de Jong provide a particularly anxious examination of state sovereignty and South African democracy in the face of an increasingly rapacious global capitalist economy (see Mackenzie, 2012). Drawing connections amongst untrammelled economic development, corrupt land reform and widening social inequalities, Mackenzie's work forms part of a broader 'post-apartheid fictional terrain' where the 'reconfigured contest over law and order' takes centre stage (de Kock, 2016, 42). This is typified by *Pale Horses*, the third of five instalments in the series, in which de Jong is called to investigate the suspicious death of Sonet Meintjies, an aid worker and base jumper who was seemingly pushed from the roof of a Johannesburg high-rise. De Jong connects Meintjies to Willaims Management, an organisation that assists in land restitution cases on behalf of dispossessed indigenous communities. Prior to her disappearance, Meintjies had been helping the Siyabonga tribe set up a sustainable farming project following a successful land claim, one that resulted in Meintjies' ex-husband losing commercial land that had been in his family 'since the Boer war' (Mackenzie, 2012, 62). When questioning the resentful Marthinus van Schalkwyk regarding his ex-wife's death, Jade fights the impulse 'to point out that indigenous communities might well have been living there for thousands of years before that', realising that, in 'Van Schalkwyk's world, history only started in 1880' (62).

It is here that Meintjies' death coincides with the text's other central mystery: the disappearance of the Siyabonga community. On speaking to Van Schalkwyk, Jade discovers that the reclaimed farmland, Doringplaas, has since transformed from a 'successful commercial maze farm' into little more than a 'desert' (Mackenzie, 2012, 63). Van Schalkwyk sees the decline of Doringplaas as evidence of the political failure of land reform to alleviate 'wrenching poverty in the country's rural areas' and uses the fate of the Siyabonga to reconfirm his own racist ideologies: '[they] trashed it – it's just a shell now. Ignorant, useless savages' (63). This prompts Jade to visit the farmland herself, where she is struck not only by the 'impossibly barren' landscape – 'as if a miniature Armageddon had taken place' – but by a deeper feeling of despair (72). Presented with apparent evidence of the inability of agricultural and political restitution to adequately transform South Africa's deeply ingrained inequalities, Jade can't help but feel that 'her own personal hopes for [the country's] future had been crushed' too (73). The relationship between Van Schalkwyk, Meintjies and the missing community would appear to point to a familial plot connecting the text's central mysteries, albeit one with roots in the nation's violent colonial past. This is seemingly confirmed by the disappearance of Meintjies' sister, Zelda, a journalist who had been writing about 'The War on Land Reform' (Mackenzie, 2012, 175). Reading Zelda's history of territorial contestation and dispossession, including details on the exclusionary zoning practices that gave shape to modern South Africa, Jade realises that 'absolute power could indeed be gained through control of a nation's agricultural resources' (176). Whilst these questions of land ownership will prove central to the text's denouement, Mackenzie ultimately shifts focus away from local 'state policies' to address the larger problem of 'global capitalism' (Guldimann, 2023, 146). In particular, *Pale Horses* examines the ways in which foreign capital and transnational trade can further compound pre-existing forms of environmental racism and injustice.

Through Zelda's investigative work, Jade discovers that, prior to their disappearance, the Siyabonga farming community had been provided with a new and highly temperamental batch of maize seed by an American corporation called Global Seeds. Unwilling to subsidise the venture – deeming it not 'remotely cost effective' – the company proposed using the farms as 'a testing ground' for new hybrid strains of genetically modified maize (Mackenzie, 2012, 244). Developed with the intention of creating a faster-growing variety of plant – uniform in size and resistant to the effects of pesticides and herbicides – the seeds were spliced with cancerous cells to promote accelerated mutation. The experimentation had disastrous consequences, with the entire community developing highly aggressive forms of stomach and intestinal cancer. Global Seeds immediately moved to 'kill the story', destroying evidence and burying the contaminated human and non-human animal bodies (Mackenzie, 2012, 254). Later questioning Danie Smit, the general manager of Global Seeds, about the cover-up, Jade realises the extent to which the financial primacies of global capitalism work only to perpetuate pre-existing inequalities. As Smit explains: 'The executives agreed [that] Siyabonga had been a very small and isolated community ... these residents had been among the country's poorest people and were, as such, not well connected to anybody in a position of power' (Mackenzie, 2012, 256). Here Jade is confronted with a newly transformed social condition, one 'that is no longer just national, just South African, but transnational in its dimensions and global in its derivations' (de Kock, 2016, 36). Under these circumstances, the structures of institutional discrimination that existed in South Africa during the apartheid take on new yet equally destructive forms. The tragic fate of the Siyabonga community can be situated in the context of what Rice, Long and Levenda term 'climate apartheid', an emerging 'system of discrimination, segregation, and violence based on various axes of oppression and privilege (race, class, gender, sexuality) that is produced by the material effects of climate change' (Rice et al., 2021, 627). As with previous or existing articulations of 'state-sponsored separateness', climate apartheid is embedded in the same practices of 'colonization, racial capitalism, and hetero-patriarchy' that, in the relentless pursuit of profit, render certain populations expendable (Rice et al., 2021, 625–629). As such, the seemingly local environmental crimes that Jade investigates are the consequence of much larger and more opaque global forces, making the once 'easier-to-define moral order of anti-apartheid struggle' inadequate in lending shape to their complexity and scale (de Kock, 2016, 42). *Pale Horses* thus shifts its attention away from local or state anxieties towards 'environmental degradation as a global issue', raising questions about the positioning of 'South Africa, and the global South' as dumping sites for failed corporate experiments and other forms of waste (Guldimann, 2023, 147). For Colette Guldimann (2023, 147), it is in this way that Mackenzie's work begins to apply 'pressure' to the traditional structures of the detective text, making it more responsive to the realities of a 'rapidly globalising world'. Guldimann (2023, 147) suggests that Mackenzie is concerned not so much with how the state redresses the violence and injustices of the apartheid but more with how the processes of political restitution are 'undermined by the devastating impact of globalised capitalism'.

Pale Horses is certainly effective in highlighting the 'imbrication of local places, ecologies and cultural practices' in larger, deterritorialised 'global networks', and, as such, usefully points to the ways in which contemporary crime fictions are attempting to represent and make comprehensible a kind of planetary environmental vision through their thematic and formal content (Heise, 2008, 210). However, such a reading is problematised by the otherwise orthodox denouement of the text, which expresses a reconsolidated conviction in the jurisdictional power of the state to reconcile and resist these multifaceted and densely interconnected global systems. Following Jade's investigation, Zelda Meintjies is eventually rescued from the clutches of paid mercenaries, with her story detailing the murder of the Siyabonga community making 'front page headlines in every major newspaper' (Mackenzie, 2012, 297). Meanwhile, a team of detectives led by Jade's on-and-off love interest Dave Patel move to arrest several senior managers at Global Seeds, along with other implicated parties from Williams Management. This exposure destroys Global Seeds' international reputation and long-term solvency, as share prices plummet on the global stock market. What *Pale Horses* presents here is a form of political reterritorialisation, where the governing power and authority of the state are reconstituted, rather than diminished, in the face of global economic pressures or threats. This 'insistence' on reconciling the complex, transnational crimes that de Jong investigates within 'clearly delineated territorial and jurisdictional limits' consolidates a somewhat orthodox vision of state governance, and thus presents an 'inadequate grasp of the complex interplay between the state and international realms in the contemporary era' (Pepper & Schmid, 2016, 7). This is particularly true of the state's capacity to identify and prosecute global or extralegal environmental crimes through the

traditional apparatus of law and order, a process that is presented here somewhat unproblematically. The text's narrative framework therefore has the
effect of regulating (and delimitating) the reader's ecological awareness
through illusions of control and order that obscure, rather than reveal, South
Africa's place within a more expansive planetary network. As Christopher
Warnes suggests, this response can be situated within the broader context of
the post-apartheid crime thriller, which, 'far from being apolitical', can be
understood as negotiating 'the threat and uncertainty that many feel to be part
of South African life, creating fantasies of control, restoration and mainten-
ance, and reflecting on the circumstances that gave rise to this unease'
(Warnes, 2012, 991). Thus, whilst *Pale Horses* can certainly be seen to offer
some perceptive insights into the 'history of colonisation and its impact on the
environment and on the indigenous peoples', these ecological preoccupations
end up being subservient to the text's 'generic conventions' (Naidu, 2014, 69).

Qiu Xiaolong's *Don't Cry Tai Lake* (Xiaolong, 2012) similarly strives to articulate the murky and entangled linkages between local crime and harder-to-grasp
transnational systems. The seventh book featuring police detective Chen Cao, the
novel extends Xiaolong's exploration of the rotten underbelly of both capitalist and
communist political systems, this time centring on the environmental destruction
perpetrated by China's barely regulated chemical and manufacturing industries. As
the text opens, Chen is vacationing at the Wuxi Cadre Recreation Centre, a luxury
resort for party officials overlooking the seemingly idyllic Tai Lake. There he
meets Shanshan, an environmental engineer at one of the chemical companies
bordering the waterfront. Shanshan reveals that factories have been dumping
industrial waste into the lake for decades, poisoning the local wildlife and leaving
the surface 'covered with a thick, foul-smelling canopy' (Xiaolong, 2012, 23).
When Chen queries how the companies have escaped prosecution, Shanshan
points to a larger state logic that prioritises instant 'economic success' above all
else: 'All they care about is the particular moment while they are here. They don't
care about what might happen in ten years, or even one year' (29). Here ecological
neglect is situated in the context of China's latest phase of economic reform, which
sees state-run companies ceding power to private, commercial interests. This is
precisely the case with Shanshan's employer, the Wuxi Number One Chemical
Company, which is due to be taken public by its corrupt general manager Liu
Deming. As the largest shareholder, Liu is set to profit considerably from the deal,
despite being directly implicated in the flagrant dumping of untreated wastewater
into the surrounding lake. When Liu is later discovered bludgeoned to death in his
office, suspicion falls on a local environmental activist suspected to have been
blackmailing company officials with public exposure of their fraudulent environmental practices.

Counter to *Pale Horses*, which personifies global capitalism in the form of a villainous multinational conglomerate, *Don't Cry Tai Lake* offers a subtler examination of its manifestations and effects. We see this not only in Xiaolong's descriptions of a 'rapidly and radically' changing Shanghai – where local businesses are being replaced by new 'stores, hotels and restaurants' built in a homogenised 'European style' – but also via his cogitations on China's moral decline (Xiaolong, 2012, 166). In one section, Chen explicitly links the rise of capitalism with the collapse of China's ethical system, suggesting that 'Confucianism' and 'Maoism' have been superseded by a new 'materialistic age' (87). This perceived decline of China's humanist and socialist traditions is signified via the avaricious capitalist Liu, a much-celebrated symbol of the country's financial reform for whom profit is 'more important than anything else' (70). In one sense, then, Chen positions the despoilment of Tai Lake as the symptom of a distinctly national crisis, where decades of 'unchecked, unbridled pollution' have left much of the fresh water in lakes and rivers around the country 'unfit to touch, let alone drink' (119). Yet he also sees these phenomena as expressions of a wider set of economic conditions, with 'human greed' the inevitable by-product of a capitalistic worldview (120). As he tells Shanshan: 'pollution isn't a problem that pertains to our country alone . . . for a three hundred percent profit, a capitalist would do anything, commit any crime, even risk being hanged' (120–121). In this way, the novel can be seen to subtly yet effectively manoeuvre between different spatial scales, highlighting, in the process, 'the ways in which places – now fluid rather than fixed – become meaningful as they merge into a larger context' (King, 2021, 1239).

This interplay between the local and the global takes on greater significance given the positioning of Xiaolong's work within the world literary marketplace. As the Chen mysteries are narratives set in China yet told for a primarily non-Chinese, English-speaking audience, the question of how to read and understand them in an era when 'literary traffic between the English and Chinese speaking world is increasing in volume, intensity and complexity' has been much debated (Hui, 2018, 47). In other words, should these texts be considered a 'new development in overseas Chinese literature', one that reflects the broader 'rise of China and its role in globalisation', or do they form part of an expanding and diverse canon of American literature (Hui, 2018, 50)? For Alan R. Velie (2009, 56), Xiaolong's work represents a quintessential example of 'the new globalized literature', as indicated by its strategic combination of 'Western critical methods' with elements of 'traditional Chinese culture'. Velie (2009, 56) stresses the presence of a decentralised cosmopolitan perspective, arguing that the texts combine 'insight into the culture and cuisine' of a rapidly transforming contemporary China together with a unique perspective on the way that Chinese literature 'is viewed in the West'. Luo Hui, on the other hand, identifies a more ambivalent 'creative impulse' at work, arguing that Xiaolong's narratives are energised less by a vague and 'celebratory new-millennium cosmopolitanism' and more by a tension between 'the limitations and possibilities [that] confront a writer who works in a foreign language [in] a rapidly globalizing world' (Hui, 2018, 47). For Hui (2018, 55), Xiaolong refuses to 'shy away from the constructs and artifices' of 'foreignness and exotism', and works to combat cliché 'through the mechanisms of deconstruction, simulation, parody and self-parody'. Thus, despite *Don't Cry Tai Lake*'s ostensible accentuation of the mobility and hybridity of culture – as typified by its numerous references to the Western traditions of detective fiction – what Hui identifies here is an equal emphasis on elements of cultural difference, reflecting, perhaps, the text's critique of 'cosmopolitanism's complicity with the logic of global capitalism' (Stević & Tsang, 2019, n.p.). The text appears deeply uncertain about the deterritorialising impacts of globalisation, and these anxieties come to inform its ultimately uneasy reconciliation of the vast and interlaced nature of environmental crime with the crime novel's normative demand for narrative closure.

Although the murder of Liu is initially suspected to be linked to the chemical company's hazardous disposal of toxic waste, it ultimately transpires to be connected to a parallel plot relating to its forthcoming initial public offering, one that implicates Lui's disgruntled former secretary-cum- mistress Mi and a resentful corporate climber called Fu. Both parties were due to profit from Liu's death and thus conspired to commit and cover up the murder. There is a moment, therefore, where the novel's ecological crimes threaten to go unattended, as underlined by the arrest of environmental activist Jiang on the unproven grounds of corporate blackmail. This is to ensure that he doesn't 'blab to the western media' about the country's corrupt environmental governance (Xiaolong, 2012, 245). As the Wuxi police chief tells Chen: 'Chinese people should be able to tell the difference between what is appropriate to discuss with the proper insiders and what one can discuss with outsiders' (245). Chen is very much one of these insiders, and it is his connection to Comrade secretary Zhao, an influential member of the party, that allows him to elevate his ecological concerns to the higher echelons of government. Zhao assures Chen that he will raise the issue at the next politburo meeting, stressing his belief that the government 'will follow a pattern of sustainable development' and won't 'leave a polluted lake to [their] children' (249).

Admittedly a less straightforward and celebratory account of bureaucratic power than presented in *Pale Horses*, the novel examines state complicity in the perpetuation of environmental crime in a way that still points to the persistence of sovereignty in some form. In other words, the text indicates that pollution, toxic dumping and other manifestations of ecological harm are still fundamentally issues of the state, and that a reconcentration of state regulation ('more state') is itself the solution. The novel only loosely connects China's fraught environmental landscape with a wider set of global dynamics, meaning that its ecological vision is still largely bound by the territorially demarcated parameters of the nation-state and by the formal confines of the police procedural. Yet, the text is also conscious of its own mimetic limitations, as indicated by Inspector Chen's parallel attempts to communicate the destruction of Tai Lake via an 'ambitious multivoiced, multiperspective poem' (Xiaolong, 2012, 98). The poem, also called 'Don't Cry Tai Lake', is conveyed to the reader in fragments over the length of the text and thus emerges as an alternative mode of narrative representation running alongside the detective novel proper. The 'disorganized' lines and realities of the poem allow Chen to structure and communicate a different kind of narrative feeling, one less hampered by the crime novel's typically limited temporal and spatial scales. It is for this reason that Chen sees poetry as 'something worth doing', despite Shanshan's claims that 'poetry can't make anything happen' (Xiaolong, 2012, 13). Staged within the novel's ostensibly orthodox formal bounds, then, is a deeper philosophical rumination on the utility of art, as well as on the broader challenge that the Anthropocene poses to our extant aesthetic modes. In this way, *Don't Cry Tai Lake* operates on two representational levels and can be seen to quietly anticipate some of the more hybridised forms of ecological crime fiction that will be discussed in Section 3.

Broken Borders and Climate Dystopias: Environmental Crime and the Deterritorialised State in *The Healer* and *Earthly Remains*

Tuomainen's *The Healer* (Tuomainen, [2010] 2014) offers a similarly useful route into thinking about contemporary crime fictions that are pushing the mode's formal boundaries via their treatment of environmental crime or catastrophe. Set in a near-future Helsinki, the novel presents a dystopian vision of ecological collapse, where untrammelled economic growth has disastrously accelerated the effects of global warming. Rising sea levels, forest fires and global pandemics are an unremarkable reality in the highly volatile terrain of the text, where some '650–800 million' climate refugees have been displaced worldwide (4). Helsinki itself is a putrefying city battered by rainfall and flash floods, prompting many of its residents to abandon their homes and move north to the new 'high security, privately owned small towns' in Canada, Sweden and Norwegian Lapland (31). With municipal services teetering on the brink of collapse, private security is now the 'only sector that is growing' (65). The text's primary mystery concerns the disappearance of protagonist Tapani Lehtinen's wife, Johanna, an investigative journalist who had been researching a series of unresolved murders attributed to a man calling himself 'The Healer'. The killer targets individuals who have contributed excessively 'to the acceleration of climate change', which, as the novel opens, already includes 'nine executives and politicians [and] their families' (12). This largely conventional murder mystery plot serves as a 'surface narrative' to a more 'overarching meta-narrative reflecting on climate change as a series of criminal actions' (Dimick, 2018).

What differentiates *The Healer* from the texts examined so far is its emphasis on the ineffectuality of the nation-state in the face of global environmental destruction. This is ostensibly examined through the localised context of Helsinki, where the near collapse of the city's bureaucratic structures forces Lehtinen to search for Johanna, and the killer, outside of the traditional channels of law enforcement. Yet Tuomainen also moves beyond these limited geographical framings, emphasising Helsinki's connection 'to the rest of the world and what is happening in it' (King, 2021, 1246). This is neatly distilled in an early section of the text when, whilst travelling on a bus through the city, Lehtinen and the reader are exposed to the wider frame of ecological upheaval via a television screen attached to the back of the driver's 'bulletproof glass' compartment (Tuomainen, [2010] 2014, 4). The almost collagic arrangement of catastrophes and conflicts that the screen displays – impacting nations as diverse as China, Spain, Italy, India and Mexico – allows for a zooming between local, regional and global scales, revealing to the reader the multifaceted and deeply imbricated nature of the climate crisis. The subsidiary effects of these ecological upheavals are also felt more materially in the rapidly changing demographic make-up of Helsinki itself, which, owing to the mass arrival of climate refugees, has 'finally become an international city', albeit not how Lehtinen 'had imagined it' (Tuomainen, [2010] 2014, 229). Stewart King points to Hamid, a displaced North African taxi driver who helps Lehtinen search for Johanna, as a 'central figure of this recent multicultural transformation', one who emphasises the text's critique of the 'focus on local concerns at the expense of global wellbeing' (King, 2021, 1246). Yet it is via Hamid that we can also begin to see the limitations of *The Healer*'s eco-cosmopolitan vision. Despite the novel's attempts to imagine less territorially situated forms of belonging through Helsinki's volatile and denationalised social terrain, it often struggles to develop a truly 'cultural perspective of the global' (Heise, 2008, 207). In particular, the dynamic between Lehtinen and Hamid emerges from what Sarah Dimick describes as 'a troubled lineage of interracial crime fighting duos', with Hamid often performing the 'brutal physical work' in protection of the 'cerebral detective' (Dimick, 2018, 27). Tuomainen therefore risks 'mapping these highly racialized roles onto the emerging politics of climate change refugees headed for Europe, assigning Lehtinen the role of protagonist while relegating Hamid to the narrative's periphery' (Dimick, 2018, 27). As such, the narrative remains largely circumscribed by the 'local scene' (and Lehtinen's field of vision), which prevents other perspectives and discourses from developing in a productive way.

On the whole, the vision of deterritorialisation that the novel presents – symptomised by the collapse of nation-states worldwide – is both violent and alienating, rather than cosmopolitan and unifying. Tuomainen certainly attempts to situate the text within a broader set of global dynamics, yet these linkages often seem too vast or opaque to be comprehended in any kind of totality. This sense of abstraction is typified by the denouement of the novel, where Lehtinen confronts the killer – an eco-radicalist called Pasi Tarkiainen – as he attempts to board a train leaving Helsinki. Held at gunpoint, Tarkiainen situates his crimes as a form of vigilante justice perpetrated against those responsible for the collapse of the world's delicate ecosystems: 'I'm on the side of good, Tapani . . .. I have to make sure that good continues to live for as long as evil and selfishness do. Maybe justice isn't winning, but it's not completely gone' (Tuomainen, [2010] 2014, 238). Tarkanian's logic of environmental justice necessitates the construction of a clear conceptual divide between climate villains and climate victims, thereby 'cracking the scale of human culpability in two' (Dimick, 2018, 31). Yet elsewhere the novel reveals human culpability to be far more dispersed and relational, thus rendering such binarised conceptualisations of guilt as fundamentally incompatible with the larger crime of climate change. This extends to Lehtinen, whose prioritisation of Johanna's safety (over all else) becomes symbolic of the forms of blinkered self-interest that produced the conditions for global ecological collapse in the first place. As one of Tarkanian's henchmen says to Lehtinen: '[H]ow many of us are truly innocent anyway?' (Tuomainen, [2010] 2014, 210).

The conclusion of the text is pervaded by bleakness and uncertainty, typified by Tarkanian's disappearance following the showdown at the train station. Lehtinen is subsequently reunited with Johanna, but the text otherwise 'spirals in resolution' (Dimick, 2018, 28). In the final pages, we learn that environmental decay continues to grow 'worse as time goes by', with little optimism for change (Tuomainen, [2010] 2014, 244). For Andrew Milner and J. R. Burgmann (2020, 127), this 'view of the planet as already inevitably and irreparably damaged is as much the stance of the novel itself' as the characters who populate it, meaning that the text knowingly leaves the reader 'bereft of social hope'. In this way, the novel channels the sense of lingering anxiety most commonly associated with 'the imperfectly finished plots' of literary noir, where both protagonist and reader are implicated in a wider sense of societal guilt (LeMenager, 2014, 136). Stewart King (2021, 1244), on the other hand, positions this resistance to closure not as a failure of 'crimate fictions' but as 'a deliberate feature', one that draws attention to the 'specific behaviours' that contribute towards climate catastrophe. As such, he suggests that *The Healer* seeks 'to raise readers' consciousness by incriminating those behaviours and attitudes that result in eco destruction', therefore expanding 'how we conceive of criminal behaviour' (King, 2021, 1244). Here King leans on a familiar critical argument often utilised when attempting to conceive of the value or utility of climate fiction; namely, that such texts help to spread awareness and/or motivate individuals to take effective action. However, the impact of climate messaging is extremely difficult to quantify in practical terms, and one cannot assume, as King seems to here, that 'educating' readers, either practically or ethically, will necessarily produce positive or constructive responses (or, indeed, that readers will actually *be* 'educated'). In his study on the efficacy of cli-fi, Mathew Schneider-Mayerson (2018, 473) found that 'most works of climate fiction' actually lead readers to 'associate climate change with intensely negative emotions, which could prove counterproductive to efforts at environmental engagement or persuasion'.

Of course, that is not to suggest that the resolutions offered by a text like *Pale Horses* are any more effectual in lending shape to the multivalent and transnational terrain of environmental harm. On the contrary, these fantasies of closure only further delimit the reader's sense of planet, as the text's environmental thematics become subservient to the crime narrative's generic demand for closure. Nonetheless, the hopelessness and doubt that pervade the final pages of *The Healer* produce an equivalent and similarly immobilising sense of narrative inertia, exposing the deep 'formal misalignments' between 'standard' crime stories and climate change (Dimick, 2018, 32). As Dimick suggests, this is particularly true of the varieties of 'scaled culpability' that climate change produces, which tend to be far more 'difficult to narrate than the paradigm of discrete culpability' that the genre ordinarily navigates (Dimick, 2018, 32). The environmental transgressions and harms that *The Healer* reveals far exceed the jurisdictional and epistemological scope of the lone investigator, disrupting the cause-and-effect relations that typically lend narrative shape to the crime novel's disorganised assembly of clues. Thus, whilst the text does strive to contextualise its local crimes within the 'larger context' of the global – and to disrupt the boundaries of the detective novel through forms of genre hybridisation – these complex dynamics still seem to elude its limited frames of reference, resulting not in new forms of eco-cosmopolitan understanding but in feelings of incomprehension, impotence and guilt (King, 2021, 1249).

At first glance, Leon's *Earthly Remains* (Leon, 2017) may not appear an obvious example of contemporary crime fictions that are forging new aesthetic templates through which to connect peoples and events across vastly different 'ecological scales' (Heise, 2008, 206). The twenty-sixth volume in her Commissario Guido Brunetti series, the novel continues Leon's focus on the local crime scenes of Venice and its surrounding lagoons, revealing a dark and murky criminal underworld behind these ostensibly picturesque landscapes. Yet the seemingly delimited spatial framing of the text belies a more complex relationship between the local and the global, one that is intimately connected to the distribution and popularity of the Brunetti mysteries within the international literary marketplace. Since the publication of *Death at La Fenice* in 1992, the series has sold over two million copies worldwide, prompting several translations, adaptations and spin-offs. Yet Leon has also received criticism for refusing to allow her works to be translated into Italian, a decision, she has argued, motivated simply 'by a desire to protect her anonymity' (McGuire, 2023, 400). For some critics, this highlights a significant tension between the ostensibly localised (Italian) settings of the novels and their largely non-Italian readership. Aina Vidal-Pérez (2023, 415), for instance, describes Leon's work as an exercise in 'ethnographic exhibitionism', arguing that the excessive concentration on descriptions of Venetian places, cuisine and social codes comes close to producing a 'touristic' gaze. What we can begin to see here is the somewhat liminal position that Leon's work occupies in relation to conventional definitions of the local and the global, which is of particular interest when considering her status as a self-proclaimed 'eco-detective writer' (Rustin, 2017). Indeed, it is *how* Leon explicitly engages with the 'subject' of environmental crime that is of primary concern to this section. Whilst *Earthly Remains* is, on the whole, largely conventional in its narrative arrangements – predominantly engaging with ecological discourses at a thematic level – its evocation of the imbricated nature of the local and the global allows for the production of a particular kind of ecological poetics. This is manifested most explicitly via Leon's representation of the laguna, which exceeds the human scale and reveals the 'deep-time environmental effects of climate catastrophe' (Vidal-Pérez, 2023, 417). However, the atemporal and borderless nature of the Laguna also means that it surpasses the territorial jurisdictions of both the detective and the state, presenting a particular challenge to the crime novel's drive for closure (as do the transnational crimes that it unearths). Thus, like *The Healer*, the novel is ultimately immobilised by the kinds of scaled culpability that it reveals, resulting in a similar sense of critical inertia.

The novel is predominantly set in Sant'Erasmo – one of the largest islands in the Venetian Lagoon – where Brunetti escapes for an extended vacation following a stress-related health scare. He is met at the villa by the custodian Davide Casati, who begins taking him out on rowing excursions around the vast tributaries of the lagoon. It is here, amongst the expanse of the salt marshes, that the reader is exposed to their first ecological crime scene, as Casati discovers that an unknown contaminant has been poisoning and destroying his carefully monitored beehives. For Casati, the environmental degradation caused by the flagrant dumping of chemical waste becomes a synecdoche for the larger failure of humanity to address its toxifying impact on the natural world: "'Look at that" .... [He'd] waved his left hand in a wide arc towards the mainland. "Everywhere, we've built and dug and tore up and done what we wanted with nature. And look at this," he'd said, turning to his right and waving out over the laguna, "we've poisoned this too"' (Leon, 2017, 157). Casati's arching gesture shifts the narrative perspective from the localised site of the lagoon to a larger planetary expanse, creating a 'circle of inclusion' that extends to non-anthropomorphic considerations such as 'animals, waters, trace elements, the air we breathe, and the soils we traverse' (McGuire, 2023, 401). As Vidal-Pérez (2023, 413) suggests, it is significant that 'the first corpse to be discovered in [the] novel is not human', indicating the text's strategic efforts to zoom outside of the localised human stories it narrates by framing them within the context of broad spatial and deep-time scales. It is these deep-time scales that prove consolation for Casati, who imagines a future for the bees beyond the parameters of the Anthropocene: 'Bees have had fifty million years [to] become what they are .... We'll never manage to kill them all. They'll survive us and what we've done to them' (Leon, 2017, 158).

The lagoon itself is central to Leon's evocation of spatial and temporal porousness and is where Casati's submerged corpse is later discovered in the aftermath of a ferocious storm. Although the man's death is deemed an accident, Brunetti is unconvinced and initiates his own investigation into the circumstances surrounding it. This leads him to Patrizia Manetti, a soil scientist who, prior to Casati's drowning, had been analysing mud samples from the poisoned beehives. Manetti was once stationed in Uzbekistan on behalf of the Food and Agriculture Organization, where she was tasked with examining the impact of the disappearing Aral Sea on the denuded lakebed. There she discovered that the vast water withdrawals needed to sustain the industrial growth of cotton had directly precipitated the draining of the sea, prompting the release of carcinogenic dusts, salts and other pesticides into the surrounding atmosphere. When she could no longer ignore the respiratory diseases and skin cancers impacting the surrounding villages, as well as the numerous 'dead animals lying in the fields', Manetti began recording these larger ecological impacts in her reports, ultimately leading to her dismissal and the suppression of her findings (182). At once pointing to the highly dispersed nature of environmental crime across traditionally demarcated geographical boundaries, the damage wrought against the Aral Sea and its surrounding communities becomes a cautionary tale for the future of the Venetian lagoon:

> 'I'm seeing how peaceful it is, how lovely the birds are, how perfectly it has evolved . . . . And I'm watching it die' . . .. She raised a hand and waved in the direction of the water . . . 'There are fewer birds – some species no longer come here to nest – there are fewer fish. I seldom see a crab in the water . . . The tides don't make sense any more . . . . [and] the earth itself . . . the earth, the planet . . . it's gone mad.' (186)

First reading the signs of ecological breakdown in the flora and fauna that surround her, Manetti ultimately expands her vision outwards, connecting these phenomena to a larger planetary derangement. For Vidal-Pérez (2023, 416), her speech operates as a kind of 'risk discourse', where 'the end of nature' is positioned as 'starting at the Venetian lagoon' before encompassing 'planet Earth as a whole'. The deterritorialised space of the lagoon becomes a symbol of such transnational connectivity, with Leon portraying how its waters 'filter [out] like tentacles from the small canals of Venice' towards 'other oceans through the polluted Mediterranean' (Vidal-Pérez, 2023, 413–416). In the process, the text exposes the inherent instability of the ideological and topographical boundaries of the nation-state, as well as the attendant problem of prosecuting environmental crime in a 'global environment' such as the lagoon, one which is almost impossible to 'regulate, inhabit and settle' (Puxan-Oliva, 2022, 42).

This is what stifles Brunetti's ability to apportion blame or enact justice. The detective comes to suspect that Casati was murdered for his attempts to expose GCM Holdings, a large petrochemical company situated in Venice's industrial region. Brunetti uncovers evidence that the company has been dumping toxic waste (meant for transportation to countries around Europe) into the waters of the lagoon for decades and that Casati had been compiling proof – via soil samples – to bring this corporate malfeasance to an end. Yet Brunetti's lack of jurisdictional power ultimately immobilises his search for truth, as does the sheer complexity and scale of the ecological crimes he is confronted with. This is neatly crystallised towards the climax of the text, when the detective tries (and fails) to make sense out of the 'anomalous' clues that confront him: 'a few dead bees in a plastic vial, the Aral Sea, two thousand euros a week, a dark mud in another vial. If they were pieces on a board, would he be able to move them round so they formed a picture?' (Leon, 2017, 226). Brunetti's inability to comprehend the larger planetary plot is rooted in his quest for culpability, which ultimately extends far beyond the particular criminal machinations of

GCM Holdings. Like *The Healer*, *Earthy Remains* ends up devolving into uncertainty, with Casati's death and GCM's crimes ultimately left unpunished. Whilst the 'intensely local nature' of *Earthly Remains* is certainly a 'red herring for the global scales of ecological (in)justice that it underlines', these global injustices are also too opaque and implausible to find meaningful shape within the traditional formal bounds of the detective novel (McGuire, 2023, 400). The result is a familiar sense of alienation, hopelessness and despair.

3 'Some New Thing': Speculative Futures and Hybrid Ecological Crime Fiction

Section 2 analysed an assortment of contemporary crime narratives cultivating new modes of representation through which to conceive of environmental crime in the context of the globe. Yet it also suggested that there are certain structural limits to the genre's capacity to effectively examine these dynamics within its extant narrative forms. This aligns with several critical works that have highlighted the scalar incompatibility between traditional variations of the crime novel and what Pepper and Schmid (2016, 8) term the 'overdetermined terrain of global capitalism', one where the state has been 'relativized as a form of political authority and locus of power'. Although not touching specifically on questions of ecology, Pepper and Schmid (2016, 15–16) suggest that it is only by 'hybridizing elements from different, but related, types of genre fiction', such as the espionage or thriller novel, that crime narratives can begin to interrogate 'the globalization of crime'. This is because such forms allow for a 'greater geographical scope', as well as a 'more expansive sense of the ways in which transnational networks of crime and policing operate in today's world' (Pepper & Schmid, 2016, 16). Marta Puxan-Oliva makes a similar claim in her discussion of contemporary ecological crime narratives, suggesting that science fiction is perhaps 'best suited to solving the scale problem of thinking at a planetary level and from a geological time frame' (Puxan-Oliva, 2020, 365). Like Pepper and Schmid, Puxan-Oliva (2020, 369) argues that the crime novel must 'push the limits of its own genre conventions' if it is to more productively address global environmental issues. This necessitates not only an expansion of the genre's 'traditional use of geographical and temporal scale' but also a questioning of its tendency 'to conform to realist conventions' (Puxan-Oliva, 2020, 369). Puxan-Oliva cites Frank Schätzing's eco-thriller *Der Schwarm* (Schätzing, 2004) – which depicts humankind's contestation with an intelligent organism that exerts control over marine life – as a text that effectively combines different genres to serve particular 'narrative purposes' (Puxan-Oliva, 2020, 365). By bringing the investigative momentum of the crime novel into contact with the textual 'strategies' of science fiction, the novel narrates 'the crimes of the Anthropocene in a temporal dimension that is uncommon to crime fiction', thus multiplying the 'stories, narrative perspectives and settings' it is able to contain (Puxan-Oliva, 2020, 365). For Puxan Oliva (2020, 365), the expansive and cross-fertilised conventions of *Der Schwarm* are what make it a 'truly global' ecological thriller.

It is these hybridised forms of crime fiction that will be the focus of this section, which will examine the capacity of such texts to offer a more productive and expansive ecological vision. Whilst certainly interrogating the ways in which hybrid crime novels enlarge the geographical, temporal and representational scope of the traditional 'realist' crime novel, this section will also explore how these texts unsettle and redirect the genre's dominant narratological orientation. What has often been overlooked in the study of ecological crime fiction is the extent to which the 'backward looking structure' of the mode is itself an inhibiting factor in the development of different, and perhaps more hopeful, environmental perspectives (Messent, 2013, 16). As Louise Hadley (2010, 60) suggests, whereas most narrative fiction is 'teleological in orientation', crime fiction, particularly the whodunit variant, typically tends 'to look backwards, and attempts to account for and reconstruct the past'. Hadley points to Tzvetan Todorov's seminal essay 'The Typology of Detective Fiction' as evidence of the ways that this reverse temporality is sedimented into the 'structural organisation' of the classic whodunit form (Hadley, 2010, 61). Yet, these formal arrangements are largely directed by the mode's deeper ideological preoccupation with apportioning guilt. In *Signs Taken for Wonders*, Franco Moretti (2020) analyses the social function of crime narratives, particularly their engagement with forms of collective and individual culpability. For Moretti, the figure of the individualised criminal – whose non-conformity absolves the larger social body of guilt – is central to the genre's ideological work: '[crime narratives] exist expressly to dispel the doubt that guilt might be impersonal, and therefore collective and social ... crime is always presented as an exception, [as] the individual must be' (Moretti, 2020, 135). For Moretti (2010, 135), the 'perfect crime', or 'nightmare of detective fiction', is the 'deindividualized crime that anyone could have committed', as then 'everyone is the same' and everyone is guilty.

Global warming is precisely this kind of 'deindividualized' crime and therefore poses a particular challenge to the genre's characteristic preoccupation with diagnosing and individualising guilt. As discussed in Section 2, this tends to catalyse contradictory yet equally inert responses from crime narratives attempting to engage with these complexities within what Pepper and Schmid describe as the mode's 'traditional' forms: those that feature 'individual protagonists, individual antagonists and specific settings (or variations thereof)' (Pepper & Schmid, 2016, 15). In a text like *Pale Horses*, climate crime is awkwardly reindividualised in the shape of the villainous corporation Global Seeds, only to be 'resolved' through delusory fantasies of state power. Even an ostensibly hybridised text like *The Healer* is still preoccupied with questions of guilt, which ultimately stifles its ability to present global environmental visions that engage awareness of crisis in a manner that exceeds the discourse of catastrophe (Heise, 2008). That is not to suggest that ecological crime narratives need offer 'happy endings' or endings that are 'definitive, satisfying or kairotic' (Johns-Putra, 2019, 166). On the contrary, the texts soon to be discussed are united by a critique of this desire for neat resolutions, which are positioned as 'unproductive' in the context of the Anthropocene (Johns-Putra, 2019, 166). Nonetheless, what separates these hybridised texts is a shift away from the crime novel's preoccupation with questions of culpability, as well as from its realist and positivist foundations. In the process, they suggest that what may be needed are not 'immobilising feelings of guilt, but a commitment towards the future', whatever that future might be (Conradie, 2011, 85).

The first subsection ('Satirical Eco-thrillers') analyses Gabriela Alemán's *Poso Wells* (Alemán, [2007] 2018) and Yun Ko-eun's *The Disaster Tourist* (Ko-eun, [2013] 2020) as examples of what I will be terming 'satirical eco-thrillers'. Whilst the narrative trajectory of the thriller form is partly what lends these texts a sense of forward momentum, it is the satiric mode, characterised by a strong inclination to produce 'a change in behaviour or attitude', that generates much of their radical and subversive energy (Knight, 2004, 205). I will focus particularly on their appeal to the conventions of the Menippean satire, a form frequently used as an instrument to 'undermine previous philosophies, or relativise them through formal play, thereby accommodating them into a new worldview' (Capoferro, 2010, 39). This is manifested most acutely through the texts' satiric subversion of the positivistic impulses synonymous with both the crime novel and the Western philosophical tradition. In the process, both texts knowingly 'refuse the equation of modernity with rationality and realism', exposing the 'breakdown of technological optimism' through the use of 'fantastic elements' and 'open plots' (LeMenager, 2014, 136). Thus, whilst not 'speculative' fictions in the traditional sense, these 'imperfectly resolved mysteries' still gesture towards the possibility of alternate worlds 'from within a genre that [has] traditionally promised closure' (LeMenager, 2014, 136). Allied with this sense of open-endedness is a subtle yet identifiable utopian impulse, one that is characteristic of the Menippean satiric tradition more broadly. However, the utopian visions offered by these novels align not with the 'classic' utopianism of 'static perfection' but with a more 'kinetic' utopianism characterised by a 'continuous process of political and social improvement' (Parrinder, 2015, 4).

The second subsection ('People Aren't the Future') examines texts that offer more explicit engagements with futurity, both within their thematic content and via their specific forms of narrative hybridisation. Focusing on *Hummingbird Salamander* by Jeff VanderMeer (2021b) and *Something New Under the Sun* by Alexandra Kleeman (2021), it suggests reading these novels as examples of what I will be terming 'speculative noir'. Whilst acknowledging, on the one hand, the ways in which these texts draw on the distinctive themes (anxiety, uncertainty, alienation) and narrative conventions (cynical protagonists, twisting mystery plots) so characteristic of the noir tradition, this designator also recognises their strategic disruption of and departure from the mode's typically pessimistic and distinctly fatalistic forms of narrative closure. Thus, while partly actualising the synchronicity between 'the darkness of ecological awareness' and the 'darkness of noir', these texts ultimately centre on questions of posterity rather than on questions of guilt (Morton, 2016, 9). Moreover, both novels shift away from distinctly anthropocentric visions of the future, opening up the possibility for 'different kinds of posterity' in the process (Johns-Putra, 2019, 167).

Satirical Eco-thrillers: Gabriela Alemán's *Poso Wells* and Yun Ko-eun's *The Disaster Tourist*

'Poso Wells does not appear on any map. How could it?' This is how Alemán ([2007] 2018, 13) introduces the reader to the fictional slum settlement of Poso Wells, a 'stinking, forgotten hole' in the depths of rural Ecuador. At once emphasising the politically deterritorialised and economically marginalised nature of the community at the centre of the text, it is an image that simultaneously foregrounds Alemán's 'preoccupation with the nature of borders' (Riofrio, 2010, 26). This not only manifests at the thematic level – where questions of gender, social class and political sovereignty will take centre stage – but can also be traced formally through *Poso Wells'* cannibalisation of various forms, genres and styles. This is a strategic move on Alemán's behalf and is expressive of her deep resistance to the rigid stratification of literary modes. As she tells Dick Cluster: 'I understand that critics need definitions [but they] only flatten out the possibilities. I love crossovers between horror and fantasy [or] social realism and poetry' (Cluster, 2018, n.p.). Acknowledging a certain 'proximity' to detective fiction as one of *Poso Wells'* many layers, Alemán also identifies the importance of 'satire' in helping the reader 'navigate the darkness at the centre of the book' (Cluster, 2018). Although Alemán uses the term satire in a general sense here, what is particularly noteworthy is the novel's appeal to the Menippean traditions of satire as defined by Mikhail Bakhtin. In *Problems of Dostoevsky's Poetics*,

Bakhtin ([1929; 1963] 1984) identifies several characteristics that distinguish the Menippean satire from other classic 'serio-comical' genres, whilst also tracing its centrality to the development of the modern European novel. Key to the ideological and aesthetic conventions of the Menippean satire is the cultivation of a 'carnival sense of the world' (Bakhtin, [1929; 1963] 1984, 113), where the carnival (as event and anarchic concept) represents 'a liberating and subversive challenge' to ideas of completeness, closure and the 'political status quo' (Ball, 2003a, 93). This is characterised by the genre's 'bold and unrestrained use of the fantastic', where 'extraordinary' situations are created for the 'provoking and testing of a philosophical idea [or] truth' (Bakhtin, [1929; 1963] 1984, 114). As such, many critics have drawn a parallel between the anti-hierarchical and anti-realist proclivities of the Menippean satire and the boundary-crossing tendencies of much postcolonial and postmodern fiction (Friedman, 2019, 16). This has a particular resonance in *Poso Wells*, where economic and ecological corruption are directly linked to the exploitative power systems of globalisation and neocolonialism.

The plot of *Poso Wells* centres on journalist Oswaldo Varas' investigation into the unexplained disappearance of several women, placing him in situ to witness various other sensational events, beginning with the extraordinary death of a corrupt presidential candidate who, during a campaign rally, is electrocuted on stage after trying to covertly urinate in his trousers. Alemán's exultant description of the event prefigures the carnivalesque energies of the novel as a whole:

> Before the wires explode and the lights go out . . . the people see the candidate rise above the stage, encircled by a celestial halo.
> Really, it's a sight to behold. Of a strange, extreme beauty. Extraordinarily so.
> And then, a smell of meat on the grill. A stench of scorched flesh that permeates every square inch of the usually vacant lot. (Alemán, [2007] 2018, 18)

Revealed here is one of the key components of the Menippean satire: the 'organic combination [of] the free fantastic with [an] extreme and crude slum naturalism' (Bakhtin, [1929; 1963] 1984, 155). The candidate's surreal, almost angelic ascension above the stage is immediately juxtaposed with the brutal realism and vulgarity of his scorched body, as Alemán works to collapse the ontological boundary between the ordinary and the incredible. His death and the phantasmic, schadenfreudic delight with which it is relayed thus represent a radical liberation from 'hierarchical fixities' and 'prevailing truths', evincing, in the process, feelings of uncertainty, change and renewal (Ball, 2003b, 99). This transformative potential is channelled most explicitly into the image of the candidate's grotesque body, which is marked by an openness and excess that, for

Bakhtin, signifies the symbolic destruction of authority and official culture. Such breakdowns in authority continue in the aftermath of this scene, when Varas witnesses the candidate's immediate successor Andres Vinueza – who is embroiled in a fraudulent deal to sell ecological reserve lands to a Canadian copper mining company – being kidnapped and taken underground by a cabal of old men 'with no eyes' (Alemán, [2007] 2018, 23). It is this ancient subterranean community that is also responsible for the abduction of the town's missing women, a reality Varas will unwittingly collide with when he stumbles across a traumatised victim in an underground tunnel network beneath the slum. Initially striving for a logical explanation that would explain the woman's presence there, Varas decides 'that no truth he was going to find would be sufficient to explain her. Or anything else' (Alemán, [2007] 2018, 59).

This positioning of truth as fundamentally inadequate in lending shape to the phantasms and abject realities of Poso Wells is indicative of Alemán's attempts to 'develop new forms of language' and 'ways of seeing' that work against 'dominant ontologies and epistemologies', particularly the 'scientific rationalism' most frequently aligned with the Western tradition of detective fiction (Holgate, 2019, 3). As John Riofrio (2010, 27) suggests, the satiric and fantastic register of *Poso Wells* should therefore be understood as a composite part of 'Alemán's fervent desire to do something [to] shake off the subtle seductiveness of inertia', as it pertains not only to forms of social, economic and ecological oppression but also to artistic modes. These energies are also traceable in Yun Ko-eun's eco-thriller-cum-surrealist satire *The Disaster Tourist* (Ko-eun, [2013] 2020), which offers a similarly caustic examination of how climate change is 'inextricably bound up with the pressures of global capitalism' (Ahmed, 2020). The protagonist of the novel is Yona Kim, a programme coordinator for a Seoul-based company called 'Jungle' which specialises in the design and delivery of tourist packages to ecological disaster zones. The increasing 'frequency and strength' of disasters around the globe and the 'resulting damage to humans and property' mean that dark tourism is now a thriving industry, as emphasised towards the beginning of the novel when Yona looks at a world map 'transformed' by annotations and coloured graphs indicating where ecological catastrophes have taken place (Ko-eun, [2013] 2020, 4). Yona faces disaster of a different kind in the early sections of the text when she is sexually assaulted by her boss, Kim. In the aftermath, she agrees to take a one month, expenses paid vacation to Mui, an island off the coast of Vietnam renowned for its large 'desert sinkhole' (24). When Yona is later separated from her tour group – and forced to stay in Mui– she realises that the island is nothing more than an elaborate 'theme park', with paid actors and constructed 'sets' designed to create the illusion of an authentic and impoverished local community (81). The site's real indigenous inhabitants are even further marginalised, forced to live offshore on 'unlicensed' shacks and stilt houses at the behest of the resort's despotic owners: a faceless multinational corporation called 'Paul' (116). Referred to disparagingly as 'crocodiles', these people are prohibited from entering the carefully curated 'tourist areas' from Monday through to Saturday, so as to keep them 'satisfactorily sanitized for the public eye' (Ju, 2020). The dissimulative, hyper-real terrain of the novel is amplified further when Yona is inculcated into a pernicious corporate scheme to script and manufacture a new 'natural' disaster, one that involves the deliberate collapse of several manmade sinkholes during an annual local festival. The motivation is ostensibly financial, with Paul hoping to benefit from an international 'disaster recovery' fund earmarked for places severely impacted by environmental catastrophes. Yet the company is also using the simulated disaster to cleanse the island of its indigenous inhabitants, all so it can take possession of the 'fertile' lands they currently inhabit.

Yona's description of Mui as an 'empty theatre [floating] on the ocean' could well be read as a synecdoche for a broader postmodern reality, one so overrun by simulation that the line between truth and fantasy has been all but distinguished (Ko-eun, [2013] 2020, 124). This collapse of conceptual boundaries is mirrored in the text's steady deconstruction of the thriller mode, as typified by Yona's strange complicity in the grotesque proceedings that surround her. Unwilling or unable to interrupt the company's oblique and multifaceted plot, Yona allows herself to be swept along by its abstract currents and uses the 'indirect' nature of her work – which involves planning the post-disaster travel programme – as justification for her inaction (150). Yona's positioning as 'protagonist' steadily fragments as a consequence, and she will eventually disappear from the narrative some twenty pages before the climax of the text, when she is killed by the company for use as a 'Mannequin' in the impending disaster. At once interrogating the relationship between myopia and the climate crisis – where a collective willingness 'to look the other way' can ultimately 'accumulate in tragedy' – here Yun Ko-eun self-consciously underlines the inadequacy of existing representational modes (crime/thriller) and literary archetypes (detective /hero) in lending meaningful shape to the absurdity of contemporary life (Buehler, 2021). For Brian McHale (2003, 172), it is this interruption of the unitary 'ontological horizon' of the 'traditional genres of official literature' that makes postmodernist fiction the 'natural heir of Menippean satire and its most recent historical avatar'. Like *Poso Wells*, *The Disaster Tourist* embraces these carnivalesque elements of hybridity and fragmentation, even if, as Madeline Leung Coleman suggests, it does sometimes risk becoming too 'oppressively real' in its satiric vision of contemporary life (Coleman, 2020). Coleman refers to Northrop Frye's discussion of satire, in which he argues that 'at least a token fantasy, a content which the reader recognizes as grotesque' is required to prevent the satire from devolving into expressions of 'puzzled defeat' ([1957] 1971, 224). Whilst the text's association of 'violence, suffering and death with black humour' is partly what negates this kind of tragic inertia, it is the ambiently utopian energies of its denouement that provide a critical alternative to the immobilising uncertainties of noir: the crime genre's most typically tragic mode (Greenberg, 2019, 222).

Before examining the denouements of both texts, and the forms of 'kinetic' utopia that they represent, it is first useful to reflect on their shared elicitation of another characteristic central to the traditions of the Menippean satire: 'the capacity to contemplate the world on the broadest possible scale' (Bakhtin, [1929; 1963] 1984, 115). Despite being set in local contexts, these novels are still eminently global crime fictions, in the sense that they make explicit connections between regional abuses, be they economic or ecological, and wider transnational forces. In particular, both texts examine how neocolonialism is tightly woven together with forms of gendered violence, racism and resource exploitation, positioning it as the primary driver behind climate change and other instances of environmental catastrophe. These dynamics are traceable in various forms throughout *Poso Wells* but embodied most explicitly in the shape of Holmes, a Canadian financier hoping to excavate Ecuador's ecologically protected cloud forest for its copper minerals. This plan is ultimately impeded by the remonstrations of 'the local, economically modest, indigenous, and mestizo residents', causing him to shift his attentions elsewhere, to a potentially lucrative land deal that would see the summit of the Andes (between Chile and Argentina) transformed into a non-taxable 'no-man's -land' for multinational mining companies (Riofrio, 2010). Although bemoaning the obstacles presented by 'peasants and environmentalists' around the world, Holmes remains confident in the broader currents of global capital (Alemán, [2007] 2018, 142–143). Towards the climax of the text, we see him planning future land acquisitions whilst travelling high above the clouds on a plane to Chile:

> He had at his disposal a map of Ecuador with all the mining deposits in a range of brilliant colours . . . .. It was just a question of time, of waiting for the right government to come to power, convincing enough investors, publicising the benefits and getting the credulous inhabitants of the country to believe in them. He could do it all in a single day's work, but not today, not now, sometime in the future (156).

All of Holmes' appearances in the novel are characterised by an acute dilation of time and space, where we find him either in transit, as in the extract above, or dislocated from temporal and spatial markers entirely. In this way, he comes to symbolise the rampant and untrammelled movement of international finance and is the means through which Alemán reveals the similar yet highly dispersed effects of these systems of power in different locations around the world. As Riofrio (2010, 30) suggests, *Poso Wells* therefore positions the exploitation of Ecuador's resources in the context of 'worldwide struggles over equality', strategically linking the 'resistance of one small community with the struggles of similar communities in Asia Africa, and the US'. *The Disaster Tourist* correspondingly situates the absurd happenings on the island of Mui within the context of these broader financial networks, thus similarly revealing 'the short-sighted cruelty' of neocolonialism (E. Kim, 2020). Underscored mostly via the detrimental impact the corporate commodification of Mui's land has on its local community, these global dynamics are also alluded to via Yun Ko-eun's engagements with questions of global waste. As the novel begins, we learn that the debris created by a recent tsunami off the west coast of South Korea has accumulated into a floating mass of plastics and 'forgettable knick-knacks' destined to 'swirl about' in the ocean for decades (Ko-eun, [2013] 2020, 2). Many predict that it might end up flowing into the notorious 'garbage island' in the Pacific Ocean, a gyre of human detritus and marine particles spanning from the west coast of North America to Japan. However, the waste returns in dramatic fashion in the closing pages, when, in something approximating poetic justice, it is swept up by an enormous tsunami that ends up engulfing the island of Mui. The planned simulated disaster is therefore superseded by a real-life ecological catastrophe, albeit one inextricably connected to human emissions and activities. Indeed, Yun Ko-eun satirises the myopia that characterises certain conservative discourses concerning anthropogenic climate change, particularly the tendency to situate human-induced environmental disasters as the consequence of 'natural' ecological cycles or shifts. We see this in a newspaper story that follows the tsunami, which claims that there was 'no human connection to the [waste's] unexpected divergence. The only explanation was a powerful wind current formed by the earth itself, an enormous flow that pushed the trash island off kilter' (180). As such, the trash island not only symbolises how the actions of one group or nation can circuitously impact the lives of another but also underlines the extent to which many of our disasters are, in some form, manufactured. The latter point is pushed to its hysterical extreme in the shape of the simulated sinkhole tragedy on Mui, yet Ko-eun is also sure to highlight the more trivial yet equally impactful manifestations of these same processes.

This apocalyptic ending to Ko-eun's novel may not, on the surface, appear to embody the elements of social utopia that Bakhtin sees as characteristic of the Menippean satire. The same could be said of the volcanic eruption that closes *Poso Wells*, which likewise conjures images of ecological cataclysm. Rafael Andúgar (2023) suggests one possible route into this, pointing to the forms of 'divine justice' – including the death of the cabal of blind men and the release of the captive women – that the eruption catalyses. Yet, and as Andúgar admits, this kind of reading also overlooks Holmes' escape from justice, not to mention the uncertain social and political terrain that the novel leaves us with. Moreover, the positioning of nature as a 'divine' force risks substantiating a nature–culture divide that only further obscures the very direct role that human activities play in many 'natural disasters', a point vividly underscored by *The Disaster Tourist*. The endings to both texts are more uncertain than this, resisting the crime genre's characteristic drive for closure and preoccupation with individualising guilt. Yet, crucially, neither do they lapse into the kind of 'lingering anxiety' that tends to define the more 'open' plots of noir fiction and film (LeMenager, 2014, 136). Rather, both commit to more cautiously optimistic visions of the future from within the otherwise uncertain worlds that they present, visions that become rooted in the principles of community and commonality. Alemán finds social and political hope in the bond forged by her three central characters, all of whom cross their stratified ideological positions in the aid of causes bigger than themselves. As Riofrio summarises: 'Varas risks his job to investigate the unexplained disappearance of scores of women ...[;] his close friend Benito ... risks his security to come to Varas's aid; and Bella, the beautiful victim of violence ...[,] refuses to remain on her side of the gender border' (Riofrio, 2010, 32). As they return in a taxi to Guayaquil in the closing pages, Alemán emphasises the obstinance and resilience of local people, telling us pointedly that 'escape did not seem to be anyone's priority in this car' (Alemán, [2007] 2018, 157). Whilst the novel clearly positions rootedness as a means of resistance against the forces of global capital, it is a form of rootedness that acknowledges the deep interconnectedness between similarly exploited peoples and communities across the globe. In this sense, *Poso Wells* is a novel 'about the many faces and places of social injustice' (Riofrio, 2010, 31). A similar vision is offered by *The Disaster Tourist* when, in the aftermath of the tsunami, we discover that the majority of the survivors are from the indigenous population of the island and were protected from the destruction by the 'ancient trees of the mangrove forest' (Ko-eun, [2013] 2020, 178). Although perhaps veering a little too close to allegory, Yun Ko-eun similarly situates localism as a counterpoint to the anaesthetising and destructive effects of untrammelled capitalism. And, like Alemán, she frames this localism within the context of a larger planetary consciousness, highlighting the inherent 'imbrication of local places, ecologies and cultural practices in global networks that reconfigure them according to [the] logic [of] deterritorialization' (Heise, 2008, 210). It is in this way that both texts can be seen to channel the utopian energies of the Menippean satire, albeit a utopianism defined not by static idealism but by a more 'kinetic' sense of 'hopeful, forward movement' (Johns-Putra, 2019, 142). Utopia, in this sense, is not an unrealistic end point but an ongoing process of social and political transformation, one that expresses hope for a changed future without obscuring the unjust and violent realities of the present. Thus, whilst not speculative narratives – as might be typically defined – both novels draw on the satiric tradition to deconstruct the positivistic foundations of the crime novel, all the while presenting open-ended mystery plots that 'suggest different outcomes and make them visible' (Cluster, 2018).

'People Aren't the Future': Ecocentric Posterity and Speculative Noir in Alexandra Kleeman's *Something New Under the Sun* and Jeff VanderMeer's *Hummingbird Salamander*

Furthering this examination of hybrid crime narratives, Alexandra Kleeman's *Something New Under the Sun* (Kleeman, 2021) is a particularly productive example of how contemporary climate narratives are employing the themes and structures of noir fiction in their interrogation of future ecological collapse. The text follows Patrick Hamlin, a middle-aged writer who travels to Hollywood to oversee the adaptation of his novel *Elsinore Lane*, an autobiographical family drama based on the 'buried trauma' of his father's death (Kleeman, 2021, 34). On meeting the film's shadowy producers, Brenda and Jay, Patrick quickly realises that his production role is not as substantial as he first imagined and that he is expected to ferry around lead actor and former child superstar Cassidy Carter. This disappointment is further compounded when he arrives on set, where he discovers that the finished screenplay bears scant resemblance to his original novel. Whilst 'the names are the same', the script has otherwise transmuted into a gaudy supernatural horror flick, literalising the more ambient and metaphorical hauntings present in the source material (Kleeman, 2021, 58). These elements of horror extend beyond the parameters of the film into Kleeman's near apocalyptic rendering of a near-future Los Angeles ravaged by urban congestion, drought and unremitting forest fires. In this highly combustible post-water landscape, the residents of California are now wholly reliant on a factory-made commercial substitute called WAT-R, which comes in a variety of price tiers and 'flavours' boasting elusive names such as WAT-R *Pure*, WAT-R *Wildly Wet* and WAT-R *Misty Morning Dew*. As Jennifer Wilson (2021) notes, the subject of water politics knowingly recalls Roman Polanski's *Chinatown* (Polanski, 1974) and is one of many conscious engagements that Kleeman makes with the traditions and conventions of noir. Patrick is particularly preconditioned by the residual power of these narratives, his expectations of Los Angeles deeply mired in stories about 'writers going to work in Hollywood and detectives tracking down the murderers of beautiful women' (Kleeman, 2021, 25). In the early sections of the text, he struggles to reconcile these cinematic fantasies with the otherwise abstract and plotless city he encounters, a space so vast and disaggregated that 'nobody can see the whole picture' (16). Growing increasingly disoriented, Patrick seeks refuge in old reruns of *Kassi Keene: Kid Detective*, an episodic TV show starring a younger Cassidy Carter as a high-school private investigator. After noticing some strange and unacknowledged recurrences between episodes, Patrick becomes immersed in an online forum called Kassi Keene Revelators, a space where dedicated fans engage in 'deep reading and analysis', searching for missing connections and hidden conspiracies beneath, or conjoining, the more customary episodic mysteries (206). The forum is particularly preoccupied with 'The Big Reveal', a plot point and 'mega narrative event' that was (they speculate) originally planned for the cancelled sixth season and would have 'cast all of Kassi's investigations in a new, darker, more unified light' (157).

This paranoid, conspiratorial logic bleeds into Patrick's experience of reality as he is confronted with a series of mysterious happenings that point to an analogous 'mega crime' exerting its influence over the city of Los Angeles. This includes the discovery of a mystery illness called ROAD (random-onset acute dementia), a form of degenerative brain disease impacting swathes of Californians across all age demographics. Patrick and Cassidy steadily transmute into pseudo detectives as together they attempt to piece together an intricate plot connecting WAT-R Corp, ROAD and the derailing production of *Elsinore Road*. Yet Kleeman uses this mystery as 'a scaffolding rather than an engine', with much of the novel's 'power' deriving from its deeper 'devotion' to the 'plot' of ecological collapse (Gunty, 2021). Whilst we see this ambiently in the smouldering wildfires surrounding the city, these themes enter the narrative more explicitly via Patrick's deteriorating relationship with his wife Alison. Early in the novel, Patrick learns that Alison and their nine-year-old daughter Nora have taken up residency at Earthbridge, a nature retreat located in the Adirondack Mountains. Rather than being geared towards conservation and sustainability, Earthbridge is centred on managing the effects of eco-grief, placing emphasis on 'mourning as the healthiest way of processing the inevitable decline of the planet' (Kleeman, 2021, 147). Alison tells the other 'Bridgers' that Patrick is in Los Angeles caring for a sick relative; her aim is to avoid 'a lecture [on] the role that Hollywood plays in celebrating the human at the expense of all else that lives and suffers' (Kleeman, 2021, 278). As Daisy

Hildyard (2021) suggests, Kleeman is particularly interested in this 'accus-ation', one that could equally be 'levelled at the tradition of the novel'. It is a propensity that *Something New Under the Sun* consciously disrupts, creating 'tensions between the intimate human stories that are the mainstay of literary fiction and the non-human worlds in which these stories happen' (Hildyard, 2021). Kleeman cultivates this perspective through an intensifying series of passages that shift the narrative focus on to what Hildyard (2021) describes as 'unseen worlds'. This includes an intense engagement not only with the minu-tiae of non-human animal and plant life – birds, cactuses, cayotes, frogs – but also with a number of inanimate and elemental existences, such as bushfires, industrial sewage pipes, cloud formations and desert fog. There is a scalar flexibility to these narrative divergences, as Kleeman moves from the moment-ary sensations of a beetle navigating the 'high-pile carpeting' in Cassidy Carter's guestroom to the deep-time scales of an ancient shoreline where 'many millions of years' of biological and geological change are mapped in a few spare sentences (Kleeman, 2021, 333, 325). In the process, Kleeman expands the otherwise 'localised' setting of the novel, constructing a planetary vision that extends to non-human 'planes of reality' (284).

These moments of 'extra reality' intrude upon the narrative with greater regularity in the latter parts of the text, as the human-centred mystery plot steadily devolves into abstraction (Hildyard, 2021). Although Cassidy and Patrick will confront the novel's ersatz villains, Brenda and Jay, about their involvement with WAT-R Corp, there is no 'big reveal' that ties the disparate elements of the text together. It is a 'mystery [that] lacks a plot' (Kleeman, 2021, 82), leaving Cassidy and Patrick grasping – much like the Kassi Keen Revelators – for some deeper and more 'unified' meaning. Soon, Patrick steadily succumbs to the amnestic effects of WAT-R, disappearing into the desert where he is later followed by a similarly deteriorating Cassidy. The concluding pages of the text then move away from these human-centred stories, offering a vision of the future that extends far beyond the scale of the Anthropocene:

> From the vantage point of the desert sand, daylight flashes on and off a thousand times in succession, strobelike . . .. Occasional fires in the distal cities, fierce rains that batter the roofs of untended homes . . . Nothing lasts until it lasts, and nothing is without its end.
>
> . . .
>
> The new flora is plasticky and hard edged: circular blooms the colour of watered-down sky, edging their way into the desert from the coast. There are chunks of concrete rubbled among real rocks, irregular shapes whose texture holds a false smoothness. Steel frames where buildings stood, tiny shards of colour indelible in the sand. When the sea rejoins the desert plains, eons have

passed and a lone bird lights on the twist of a bough, a bird of different shape. Pale-skinned whales breach where towering cliffs had stood, reptile-fish flash bright in the shallows . . . . The sun rises and sets in the long after, without name or recognition. (Kleeman, 2021, 350)

Kleeman's prose emulates the effect of time-lapse photography, revealing a planetary surface unmade and remade by a coalescing current of climatic, geological and biological forces. The remnants of the Anthropocene are 'rubbled' into abstract shapes and forms, becoming the fossils of a future not yet known. Disrupting the typical spatial and temporal discontinuities of the (crime) novel, this evocation of deep time forces a delineation between the end of *our* world and the end of *the* world. It is a vision of the future palpably devoid of the doom and anxiety that permeate the text elsewhere, as Kleeman redirects the uncertainty and open-endedness of noir towards a more radical, ecocentric 'ethics of posterity; that is, the application of moral considerability to the future of ecosystems, and their species' (Johns-Putra, 2019, 27). As such, the novel concludes with an acknowledgement not only that 'endings do not bring neatly resolved meanings' but, more significantly, that 'the future need not resemble us' (Johns-Putra, 2019, 167). As Nora tells her friends at Earthbridge, perfectly distilling the divergent energies of speculative noir: 'People aren't the future' (Kleeman, 2021, 276).

Such radical conceptualisations of posterity are traceable in VanderMeer's *Hummingbird Salamander* (2021b), a speculative thriller that similarly draws on the aesthetic traditions of noir in its evocation of a near-future climate dystopia. VanderMeer's work is commonly associated with the stylistic heterogeneity of the 'new weird', a 'type of urban, secondary-world fiction that subverts the romanticized ideas about place found in traditional fantasy' (VanderMeer, 2008, xvi). For VanderMeer, the strategic breakdown of literary genres is what makes the 'new weird' particularly adept at capturing the disorientation of environmental change on a planetary scale. Here VanderMeer's work aligns closely with that of Timothy Morton, who likewise situates the 'weird' as a useful 'ontological category' for conceptualising the 'twisted, looping' nature of ecological awareness (Morton, 2016, 6). It is this grappling with the 'ontological strangeness' of Anthropocene realities that Louise Economides and Laura Shackelford see as a key marker of VanderMeer's work, typified by his formal merging of 'established realist genres' with elements of 'fantasy, horror and speculative fiction' (Economides & Shackelford, 2021, 3). Whilst identifying a political bent behind this formal experimentation – arguing that VanderMeer's fictions are designed to 'jar us out of complacency' – they also point to the broader incompatibility of realism with a contemporary reality where 'there is no quotidian, habitual background to rely on' (Economides & Shackelford, 2021, 3, 4). Rather than 'distorting' the real,

VanderMeer's work shows us that 'ontological reality in the 21st century is always already surreal' (Economides & Shackelford, 2021, 4).

Described by VanderMeer as 'a thriller-mystery set ten seconds into the future' (Gardiner, 2021), *Hummingbird Salamander* follows Jane Smith, a six-foot-tall suburban mum and former high-school wrestler who works as a 'vulnerability analyst' for a cybersecurity firm (Gardiner, 2021). Jane is thrown into the unlikely role of detective when she receives an anonymous note, one that leads her to a storage unit containing the taxidermied body of an extinct hummingbird. It was left to Jane by Silvina Vilcapampa, a missing corporate heiress turned eco-radicalist with links to environmental and animal rights extremist groups. As Jane is swept through this murky underworld of corporate espionage, wildlife smuggling and bioterrorism, she slowly unravels a secret connecting Silvina to her own traumatic past. The novel is structured as a written testimony, bearing the stylistic traces of the kind of confessional and fatalistic narrative forms commonly associated with the tradition of noir fiction. This sense of creeping inexorability is heralded in the prologue, where, as well as portending her own death, Jane clarifies that she 'is here to show [us] how the world ends' (VanderMeer, 2021b, 2). Such narrative and aesthetic borrowing extends to Jane's narrative voice, which channels the 'snappy, poetic weariness of the hardboiled' detective (Brookins, 2021). These conventions are explicitly acknowledged by Jane, who describes her search for truth as being dependent on her capacity to see 'things from the point of view of the private eye' (VanderMeer, 2021b, 113). This necessitates the development of a 'paranoid' worldview, as well as an acceptance of her own complicity in the degradation that surrounds her (113). Like *The Healer*, *Hummingbird Salamander* unfolds against the backdrop of global ecological collapse, where failed nation-states, pandemics and extreme weather events now constitute the fabric of contemporary life. Jane is initially inured to these everyday horrors, more inclined to focus on the 'ways life was better, even if the world wasn't' (VanderMeer, 2021b, 41). Yet the search for Silvina steadily brings Jane to an awareness of her own 'fatal adaptation' (35), particularly as it pertains to the 'ongoing, everyday exhibit of dead animals and their parts' (98). She comes to perceive not only just 'how many dead things haunt us in our daily lives' but also how our minds are trained to render these mass atrocities as 'setting' (98). As these complex and 'hidden lines of connection' slowly begin to emerge, Jane wonders: 'How did I not see the damage for so long?' (99).

Part of what the novel is attempting to reveal is the extent to which 'humans are connected to the rest of nature, even when we'd rather not think about it' (Berlatsky, 2021, n.p.). Within this, exposing the horror of mass animal death is as much an aesthetic concern as a thematic one. In an article on his personal website, VanderMeer points to the work of nineteenth-century German naturalist

Alexander Von Humboldt as a key inspiration behind the novel's composition, particularly his 'Naturgemalde', a revolutionary painting of nature that emphasises the interrelations amongst all forms of life. For VanderMeer (2021a), it is the responsibility of writers to keep in mind some version of this precept, to reveal the 'complexities of ecosystems' and translate them formally into narratives that 'incorporate useful granularity without lapsing into the didactic'. This involves drawing a distinction between 'information' and 'story', as shown through VanderMeer's juxtaposition of the language of scientific discourse, such as in the 'inserted' descriptions of a hummingbird's anatomical features and migration patterns, with Jane's deepening immersion in the horrifying lived realities of the animals being systematically destroyed around her. The influence of Von Humboldt is similarly traceable in the political and architectural logics of Unitopia, a sustainable environmental community founded by the missing Vilcapampa. Constructed out of recycled plastics, the centre was initially designed as an eco-artists' commune oriented towards cultivating sensitivities to the natural world's various forms of communication, particularly those exceeding our 'primitive five senses' (VanderMeer, 2021b, 170). Searching the abandoned commune, Jane discovers not only a graphic displaying 'sedimentary layers within the earth and levels above' but also a manifesto speculating on what could be accomplished 'if we could truly see the hidden underpinnings of the world' (169). The manifesto imagines a future where, through either an 'immersive virtual reality or other method', humans are able to perceive the most subtle environmental shifts, down to the 'chemical signals in the air from beetles and plants' or the 'pheromone trails laid down by ants' (170). Initially interpreting this as an aesthetic philosophy, an endeavour to alter human perception through art, Jane later uncovers a more complex ecological conspiracy connecting Silvina and Unitopia with bioterrorism. Prior to this, her search for truth will meander itinerantly over several years, as she tries (and fails) to uncover a master narrative connecting the varying and intensifying symptoms of ecological collapse. Yet climate change is not solvable within the traditional parameters of the detective novel, leaving Jane chasing 'even staler breadcrumbs, convinced that just one more clue [will] bring [her] the solution' (278). In the process, she abandons her husband and daughter, sacrificing the obligations of home and family in commitment to a different, more radical ethics of posterity. In this way, the novel disrupts what Johns-Putra describes as the idealisation of 'posterity as parenthood', where the 'obligation to future generations' is typically situated as the very basis for environmental action (Johns-Putra, 2019, 7, i). Like *Something New Under the Sun*, it instead advocates for an alternate form of environmental ethics, one where this responsibility to the future – a future that is, in essence, unknowable – is conceived outside of, or beyond, anthropocentric considerations.

This is cemented at the climax of the novel, when Jane discovers the body of Silvina in an underground bunker inside an excavated mountain. Prior to her death, Silvina had been working on a 'magic elixir' made from the 'defensive toxins' produced by salamanders and the 'alkaloids in flowers preferred by the hummingbird', one that would theoretically harness 'their power' and produce in humans 'a new, true seeing' (VanderMeer, 2021b, 343). Knowing that the serum might kill her, she constructed a fail-safe within the body of the mountain, an artificial micro-habitat of animal and plant life to be released into the outside atmosphere a century into the future (345). On discovering Silvina's work, Jane injects herself with the one remaining vial of elixir, figuring that it is 'worth the price' to 'change the world', even if she dies in the process (348). 'I may not know what happens next. Or even recognize it,' she says in the final moments of the narrative, leaving her own fate and that of the planet entirely unresolved (349). Through this sacrifice, Jane commits to a radical ecocentric ethics of posterity, where the 'moral considerability to the future of ecosystems and their species' is placed above all else (Johns-Putra, 2019, 27). Unlike Kleeman, VanderMeer stops short of contemplating what this future might look like, acknowledging that such a world likely exceeds our imaginative capacities and existing narrative frameworks. Jane is left pondering these uncertainties, unsure if she and the planet are shuttling inexorably towards death or if they will emerge again as 'some new thing' (VanderMeer, 2021b, 349). Whilst embracing uncertainty, then, the denouement to VanderMeer's 'speculative noir' resists the straight pessimism and negativity most frequently associated with the noir mode, with the 'open plot' instead impelling the reader into 'a kind of production' (LeMenager, 2014, 136). This is cultivated not only through Jane's direct address to the reader in the final lines but also through VanderMeer's use of paratextual elements throughout, such as a series of inserted images that appear at various section breaks throughout the novel. Whilst some of these refer to real sources, such as the image of Von Humboldt's 'Naturgemalde', others expand upon the fictional world of the text, as exemplified by the architectural blueprint for Unitopia. VanderMeer's affiliated websites similarly encourage further narrative engagement, as well as forms of participatory activism.[1] The novel thus stands as a powerful call to action, at both a political and an aesthetic level.

Conclusion: Plotting Against Climate Change

This Element has been structured around a fairly simple provocation: that there are certain limits to the crime novel's capacity to accommodate and interrogate

---

[1] See https://friendsofsilvina.com and https://unitopia.live/.

the scales and complexities of the climate crisis within its 'traditional' generic forms (i.e., realist narratives that feature a single detective investigating a single crime within a geographically and temporally enclosed setting). It is a provocation that has been designed by no means to denigrate, devalue or dismiss the genre's historical, cultural or aesthetic value but rather to serve as the basis for an investigation into the ways in which contemporary ecological crime narratives are cultivating new forms of environmental awareness through textual strategies that connect the local, the national and the global. In this sense, this study forms part of a broader critical questioning – within the fields of both ecocriticism and the environmental humanities – of the role that our existing cultural and artistic forms (particularly, in this case, 'popular' modes such as genre fiction) can play in fostering more adequate understandings of and responses to the global climate crisis. How, in other words, is literature attempting to plot against climate change? It is a subject that is still largely underexplored in the context of crime fiction studies, and one of the aims of this Element has been to bring such discourses into a more direct and urgent dialogue with some of the excellent recent work that has been undertaken in the arena of world crime fiction. This has been reflected in my methodological approach, which has not only analysed the particular formal or aesthetic arrangements that writers of crime fiction are cultivating in their textual representations of the immense and knotted nature of climate change – rather than, say, focusing on a specific set of thematics – but also endeavoured to move beyond a focus on national literatures through a comparative practice that has drawn connections between texts from across the globe. Part of the intention behind this expanded geographical focus has been to contribute towards the critical dismantling of the Anglo-American 'grand narrative' that has tended to dominate critical discussions of the genre's development, instead pointing to its continued reinterpretation and adaptation across a range of borders. There are drawbacks to this approach, of course; some of the readings here are no doubt inhibited by my own linguistic limitations and I am certainly indebted to the several excellent translations that have allowed me to expand the critical frame of this work beyond anglophone literatures. Within this, there is always a balance to be struck between the particularities of individual texts and the broader connections – or points of continuity – that one is attempting to foster between them, and it is my hope that any deficiencies in regard to the former are duly compensated for by the strengths of the latter.

The texts selected here are, of course, by no means an exhaustive representation of contemporary ecological crime fictions; there are undoubtedly innumerable more examples, perhaps some that even counter, destabilise or entirely deconstruct the arguments I have assembled across the length of this Element.

Further research is very much welcome in any case, and I in no way see this Element as a definitive examination of the subject at hand. As mentioned in the Introduction, this project was not conceived as a history or survey of ecological crime fiction, and there has been no attempt here to map a chronology of its formal development or to delineate a particular set of conventions or tropes. On the contrary, I have looked to interpret the field of ecological crime fiction as a kind of reading practice, a way of thinking about the crime genre as a whole rather than as a subgenre with its own specific histories, traditions and touch-stones. Conceiving of it as method, rather than mode, not only helps prevent new hierarchies and forms of canonisation from emerging but also allows for the reading of works where ecological preoccupations might be more latent or occluded in their thematic or formal content. Of course, some crime fictions may still be more obviously or consciously ecological than others (as the majority of the texts studied here have shown), but I remain reluctant – for the reasons provided – to treat such works as manifestations of a separate branch of crime writing proper. In this way, we are able to open up the possibilty for an entirely new way of conceiving of the genre's histories and forms, emphasising how, in one way or another, crime fiction has always been inherently ecological.

Before bringing this short addendum to an end, it is perhaps apt to return to the question of resolutions, a subject that has preoccupied much of the critical discussion in this Element. Given the crime genre's close proximity to the historical development and constitutive logics of Western modernity – and given that anthropogenic climate change is largely the consequence of the energy systems that enabled the large-scale industrialisation of societies – part of what this Element has looked to investigate is whether crime fictions need imagine different forms of resolution, ones that perhaps work against the principles of logic, reason and mastery that have long undercut both the genre and Western intellectual thought at large. The impression that all crime fictions must offer neat resolutions to the mysteries they present, or somehow work to maintain an ingrained status quo, rests on an assumed political conservatism underpinning the history and traditions of the mode, when, in truth, crime fiction has always moved variably between positions of radicalism and orthodoxy (Pepper, 2016, 2). Moreover, and as examined in Section 2, crime novels that offer overly neat resolutions to a complex series of global, environmental and political entanglements may only work to 'reinforce cultural inertia rather than challenging it' (Murphy, 2023, 237). Conversely, then, and as pointed to in my examination of hybridised crime novels, perhaps it is only by embracing open-endedness or by actively working against the expectations of plot that we can begin to meaningfully unpick the complexity and capaciousness of our world systems, that we can begin to imagine different kinds of future.

Works Cited

Ahmed, S. (2020) "*The Disaster Tourist* by Yun Ko-eun Review – Life Under Late Capitalism." *Guardian*, 9 July. Available at: www.theguardian.com/books/2020/jul/09/the-disaster-tourist-by-yun-ko-eun-review-life-under-late-capitalism.

Alemán, G. ([2007] 2018) *Poso Wells*. Translated by D. Cluster. San Francisco, CA: City Lights Books. Originally published in Spanish. Quito: Eskeletra.

Allan, J. et al. (2020) "Introduction: New Directions in Crime Fiction Scholarship." In J. Allan et al., eds., *The Routledge Companion to Crime Fiction*. Abingdon: Routledge, pp. 1–9.

Anderson, B. (2006) *Imagined Communities*. London: Verso.

Andúgar, R. (2023) "Environmental Crime and the Dialectics of Slow and Divine Violence in *Poso Wells* by Gabriela Alemán." In N. Ashman, ed., *The Routledge Handbook of Crime Fiction and Ecology*. New York: Routledge, pp. 165–176.

Ashman, N. (2018) "Hard-Boiled Ecologies: Ross Macdonald's Environmental Crime Fiction." *Green Letters: Studies in Ecocriticism*, 22(1), 43–54.

Ashman, N. (ed.) (2023) *The Routledge Handbook of Crime Fiction and Ecology*. New York: Routledge.

Avery, K. and Nelson, P. (2016) *It's All One Case: The Illustrated Ross Macdonald Archives*. Seattle, WA: Fantagraphics Books.

Bakhtin, M. M. ([1929; 1963] 1984) *Problems of Dostoevsky's Poetics*. Translated by C. Emerson. Minneapolis: University of Minnesota Press. Originally published in 1929 in Leningrad as *Problems of Dostoevsky's Creative Art* (Проблемы творчества Достоевского, *Problemy tvorčestva Dostoevskogo*) but republished with significant additions under the new title in 1963 in Moscow.

Ball, J. C. (2003a) "Pessoptimism: Satire and the Menippean Grotesque in Rushdie's *Midnight's Children*." In R. Mittapalli and J. Kuortti, eds., *Salman Rushdie: New Critical Insights*. New Delhi: Atlantic.

Ball, J. C. (2003b) *Satire and the Postcolonial Novel: V. S. Naipaul, Chinua Achebe, Salman Rushdie*. New York: Routledge.

Berlatsky, N. (2021) "Review: Climate collapse comes for the spy thriller in Jeff VanderMeer's sly genre game." *Los Angeles Times*, 3 March. Available at: www.latimes.com/entertainment-arts/books/story/2021-03-30/review-climate-collapse-comes-for-the-spy-thriller-in-jeff-vandermeers-sly-genre-game.

Bolados García, P. (2023) "Resistance of Women from 'Sacrifice Zones' to Extractivism in Chile: A Framework for Rethinking a Feminist Political Ecology." In B. Bustos et al., eds., *Routledge Handbook of Latin America and the Environment*. Abingdon: Routledge, pp. 207–214.

Brookins, J. C. (2021) "Investigating the Anthropocene in 'Hummingbird Salamander'." *Chicago Review of Books*, 14 April. Available at: https://chireviewofbooks.com/2021/04/14/investigating-the-anthropocene-in-hummingbird-salamander/.

Buehler, L. (2021) "Yun Ko-eun: Into the Wreckage." *Bookanista*, n.d. Available at: https://bookanista.com/yun-ko-eun/.

Buell, L. (2007) "Ecoglobalist Affects: The Emergence of U.S. Environmental Imagination on a Planetary Scale." In W. C. Dimock and L. Buell, eds., *Shades of the Planet: American Literature as World Literature*. Princeton, NJ: Princeton University Press, pp. 227–248.

Capoferro, R. (2010) *Empirical Wonder: Historicizing the Fantastic, 1660–1760*. Bern: Peter Lang.

Clark, T. (2015) *Ecocriticism on the Edge: The Anthropocene as a Threshold Concept*. London: Bloomsbury.

Clark, T. (2019) *The Value of Ecocriticism*. Cambridge: Cambridge University Press.

Cluster, D. (2018) "Literature Is the Minefield of the Imagination: An Interview with Gabriela Alemán." *Los Angeles Review of Books*, 17 July. Available at: https://lareviewofbooks.org/article/literature-is-the-minefield-of-the-imagination-an-interview-with-gabriela-aleman/.

Coleman, M. L. (2020) "This Is What Happens When Society 'Has to Function'." *The Atlantic*, 13 August. Available at: www.theatlantic.com/culture/archive/2020/08/disaster-tourist-yun-ko-eun-capitalist-satire-pandemic-work/615151/.

Conradie, E. M. (2011) "Confessing Guilt in the Context of Climate Change: Some South African Perspectives." In S. Bergmann and H. Eaton, eds., *Ecological Awareness: Exploring Religion, Ethics and Aesthetics*. Berlin: LIT Verlag, pp. 77–98.

Crichton, M. (2004) *State of Fear*. New York: HarperCollins.

Damrosch, D. (2018) *What Is World Literature?* Princeton, NJ: Princeton University Press.

De Kock, L. (2016) *Losing the Plot: Crime, Reality and Fiction in Postapartheid South African Writing*. Johannesburg: Wits University Press.

De Manuel, J. (2006) *L'olor de la pluja [The Smell of Rain]*. Barcelona: La Mangrana.

Dhillon, K. (2022) *Indigenous Resurgence: Decolonialization and Movements for Environmental Justice*. New York: Berghahn Books.

Dimick, S. (2018) "From Suspects to Species: Climate Crime in Antti Tuomainen's *The Healer*." *Mosaic*, 51(3), 19–35.

Disher, G. (2013) *Bitter Wash Road*. Melbourne, VIC: The Text Publishing Company.

Duckert, L. (2021) "Coal/Oil." In J. Cohen and S. Foote, eds., *The Cambridge Companion to Environmental Humanities*. Cambridge: Cambridge University Press, pp. 214–228.

Economides, L. and Shackelford, L. (2021) "Introduction – Weird Ecology: VanderMeer's Anthropocene Fiction." In L. Economides and L. Shackelford, eds., *Surreal Entanglements: Essays on Jeff VanderMeer's Fiction*. New York: Routledge, pp. 1–26.

Erdmann, E. (2009) "Nationality International: Detective Fiction in the Late Twentieth Century." In M. Krajenbrink and K. Quinn, eds., *Investigating Identities: Questions of Identity in Contemporary International Crime Fiction*. Amsterdam: Rodopi, pp. 11–26.

Fakhrkonandeh, A. (2022) "Oil Cultures, World Drama and Contemporaneity: Questions of Time, Space and Form in Ella Hickson's *Oil*." *Textual Practice*, 36(11), 1775–1811.

Fetherston, R. (2023) "Unsettlement, Climate and Rural/Urban Place-Making in Australian Crime Fiction." In N. Ashman, ed., *The Routledge Handbook of Crime Fiction and Ecology*. New York: Routledge, pp. 78–90.

Follett, A. (2023) "Oil and the Hardboiled: Petromobility, Settler Colonialism and the Legacy of the American Century in Thoams King's *Cold Skies*." In N. Ashman, ed., *The Routledge Handbook of Crime Fiction and Ecology*. New York: Routledge, pp. 374–386.

Friedman, A. L. (2019) *Postcolonial Satire: Indian Fiction and the Reimagining of Menippean Satire*. Lanham, MD: Lexington Books.

Frye, N. ([1957] 1971) *Anatomy of Criticism: Four Essays*. Princeton, NJ: Princeton University Press.

Gardiner, M. (2021) "Jeff VanderMeer Talks Noir, Suspense, and His New Eco-thriller." *CrimeReads*, 25 February. Available at: https://crimereads.com/jeff-vandermeer-meg-gardiner/.

Ghosh, A. (2016) *The Great Derangement: Climate Change and the Unthinkable*. Chicago, IL: University of Chicago Press.

González, A. E. (2020) "Ghosts in a Machine: On Fernanda Melchor's 'Hurricane Season.'" *Cleveland Review of Books*, 8 December. Available at: www.clereviewofbooks.com/writing/2020-12-8-on-fernanda-melchors-hurricane-season.

Goodbody, A. and Johns-Putra, A. (2019) *Cli-Fi: A Companion*. Oxford: Peter Lang.

Greenberg, J. (2019) *The Cambridge Introduction to Satire*. Cambridge: Cambridge University Press.

Gulddal, J. and King, S. (2022) "What Is World Crime Fiction?" In J. Gulddal et al., eds., *The Cambridge Companion to World Crime Fiction*. Cambridge: Cambridge University Press, pp. 1–24.

Gulddal, J. et al. (eds.) (2019) *Criminal Moves: Modes of Mobility in Crime Fiction*. Liverpool: Liverpool University Press.

Gulddal, J. et al. (eds.) (2022) *The Cambridge Companion to World Crime Fiction*. Cambridge: Cambridge University Press.

Guldimann, C. (2023) "Protecting the Rhinos and Our Young Democracy: Nature and the State in Post-Apartheid South African Crime Fiction." In N. Ashman, ed., *The Routledge Handbook of Crime Fiction and Ecology*. New York: Routledge, pp. 141–152.

Gunty, T. (2021) "A Thirst That Big: On Alexandra Kleeman's 'Something New Under the Sun'." *Los Angeles Review of Books*, 20 September. Available at: https://lareviewofbooks.org/article/a-thirst-that-big-on-alexandra-kleemans-something-new-under-the-sun/.

Hadley, L. (2010) *Neo-Victorian Fiction and Historical Narrative*. London: Palgrave.

Halla, B. (2020) "Barbara Halla Reviews *Hurricane Season* by Fernanda Melchor." *Asymptote*, n.d. Available at: https://shorturl.at/3DAZf.

Harper, J. (2016) *The Dry*. Sydney, NSW: Macmillan Australia.

Haverty Rugg, L. (2017) "Displacing Crimes Against Nature: Scandinavian Ecocrime Fiction." *Scandinavian Studies*, 89(4), 597–615.

Heise, U. K. (2008) *Sense of Place and Sense of Planet: The Environmental Imagination of the Global*. Oxford: Oxford University Press.

Heise, U. K. (2013) "Globality, Difference, and the International Turn in Ecocriticism." *PMLA (Publications of the Modern Language Association)*, 128(3), 636–643.

Hildyard, D. (2021) "Something New Under the Sun by Alexandra Kleeman Review – Hollywood Apocalypse." *Guardian*, 11 August. Available at: www.theguardian.com/books/2021/aug/11/something-new-under-the-sun-by-alexandra-kleeman-review-hollywood-apocalypse.

Holgate, B. (2019) *Climate and Crises: Magical Realism as Environmental Discourse*. Abingdon: Routledge.

Hollister, L. (2019) "The Green and the Black: Ecological Awareness and the Darkness of Noir." *PMLA (Publications of the Modern Language Association)*, 134(5), 1012–1027.

Hui, L. (2018) "Shanghai, Shanghai: Placing Qiu Xiaolong's Crime Fiction in the Landscape of Globalized Literature." In J. Anderson et al., eds., *The Foreign in International Crime Fiction: Transcultural Representations*. New York: Continuum, pp. 47–59.

Hutchinson, B. (2018) *Comparative Literature: A Very Short Introduction*. Oxford: Oxford University Press.

Janson, J. (2022) *Madukka the River Serpent*. Crawley, WA: UWA Publishing (e-book).

Johns-Putra, A. (2019) *Climate Change and the Contemporary Novel*. Cambridge: Cambridge University Press.

Ju, S. (2020) "Too Close to Home: On Ko-eun's *The Disaster Tourist*." *Los Angeles Review of Books*, 4 August. Available at: https://lareviewofbooks .org/article/too-close-to-home-on-yun-ko-euns-the-disaster-tourist/.

Kavanagh, B. (2020) "A Colonial Settlement Story from the Indigenous Point of View." Sydney Morning Herald, 13 June. Available at: www.smh.com.au/ culture/books/a-colonial-settlement-story-from-the-indigenous-point-of-view-20200604-p54zja.html.

Kim, E. (2020) "Yun Ko-eun's 'The Disaster Tourist'." *White Review*, September. Available at: www.thewhitereview.org/reviews/yun-ko-euns-the-disaster-tourist/.

Kim, J. H. (ed.) (2020) *Crime Fiction and National Identities in the Global Age: Critical Essays*. Jefferson, NC: McFarland & Company.

King, S. (2011) "Detecting Difference/Constructing Community in Basque, Catalan and Galician Crime Fiction." In N. Vosburg, ed., *Iberian Crime Fiction*. Cardiff: University of Wales Press, pp. 51–74.

King, S. (2021) "*Crimate* Fiction and the Environmental Imagination of Place." *Journal of Popular Culture*, 54(6), 61–71.

King, S. (2023) "Indigenous Crime Fiction Is Rare, but in Madukka the River Serpent Systemic Violence and Connection to Country Are Explored." *Yahoo! News* (republished from *The Conversation*), 20 March. Available at: https://au.news.yahoo.com/indigenous-crime-fiction-rare-madukka-045514821.html.

King, T. (1993) *Green Grass, Running Water*. Montreal, QC: Houghton Mifflin Company.

King, T. (1999) *Truth and Bright Water*. Toronto, ON: HarperFlamingo Canada.

King, T. (2018) *Cold Skies*. Toronto, ON: HarperCollins.

Kleeman, A. (2021) *Something New Under the Sun*. London: 4th Estate.

Knight, C. A. (2004) "Satire and the Novel." In C. A. Knight, *The Literature of Satire*. Cambridge: Cambridge University Press, pp. 203–232.

Ko-eun, Y. ([2013] 2020) *The Disaster Tourist*. Translated by L. Buehler. London: Serpent's Tale. Originally published in Korean as 밤의 여행자들 (Travelers of the Night). Seoul: Minumsa.

Krajenbrink, M. and Quinn, K. M. (eds.) (2009) *Investigating Identities: Questions of Identity in Contemporary International Crime Fiction*. Amsterdam: Rodopi.

Leichenko, R. M. and O'Brien, K. L. (2008) *Environmental Change and Globalization: Double Exposures*. Oxford: Oxford University Press.

LeMenager, S. (2014) *Living Oil: Petroleum Culture in the American Century*. Oxford: Oxford University Press.

Leon, D. (2017) *Earthly Remains*. London: Arrow.

Lerner, S. (2010) *Sacrifice Zones: The Front Lines of Toxic Chemical Exposure in the United States*. Cambridge, MA: MIT Press.

Locke, A. (2009) *Black Water Rising*. London: Serpent's Tail.

Macdonald, G. (2017) "Monstrous Transformer: Petrofiction and World Literature." *Journal of Postcolonial Writing*, 53(3), 289–302.

Macdonald, R. (1973) *Sleeping Beauty*. New York: Knopf.

Mackenzie, J. (2012) *Pale Horses*. New York: Soho Crime.

Manning, P. M. (2024) "The Climate of Indigenous Literature: Thomas King's Anthropocene Realism." *Critique: Studies in Contemporary Fiction*, 65(1), 33–50.

Matzke, C. and Mühleisen, S. (2006) "Introduction: The Anatomy of Crime." In C. Matzke and S. Mühleisen, eds., *Postcolonial Postmortems: Crime Fiction from a Transcultural Perspective*. Amsterdam: Rodopi, pp. 1–16.

McGuire, V. (2023) "Reading Donna Leon as Mediterranean Noir." In N. Ashman, ed., *The Routledge Handbook of Crime Fiction and Ecology*. New York: Routledge, pp. 399–409.

McHale, B. (2003) *Postmodernist Fiction*. Abingdon: Routledge.

Mclean, G. (2014) *Wolf Creek*. Melbourne, VIC: Penguin Books Australia.

Melchor, F. (2017) *Hurricane Season*. London: Fitzcarraldo.

Messent, P. (2013) *The Crime Fiction Handbook*. Hoboken, NJ: Wiley.

Milner, A. and Burgmann, J. R. (2020) *Science Fiction and Climate Change: A Sociological Approach*. Liverpool: Liverpool University Press.

Morales Hernández, L. C. (2022) *Geographies of Violence and Extraction in the Cultural Production of the Mexican Late Neoliberal Period*. PhD thesis, King's College London. https://kclpure.kcl.ac.uk/ws/portalfiles/portal/181949726/2022_Morales_Hernandez_Lya_1717380_ethesis.pdf.

Moretti, F. (2020) *Signs Taken for Wonders: Essays in the Sociology of Literary Forms*. London: Verso.

Morton, T. (2016) *Dark Ecology: For a Logic of Future Coexistence.* New York: Columbia University Press.

Murphy, P. D. (2009) *Ecocritical Explorations in Literary and Cultural Studies: Fences, Boundaries, and Fields.* Lanham, MD: Lexington Books.

Murphy, P. D. (2023) "In Paulo Bacigalupi's Environmental Science Fiction, Immoral and Criminal Acts Are Not Synonymous." In N. Ashman, ed., *The Routledge Handbook of Crime Fiction and Ecology.* New York: Routledge, pp. 228–238.

Nadasdy, P. (2005) "Transcending the Debate over the Ecologically Noble Indian: Indigenous Peoples and Environmentalism." *Ethnohistory*, 52(2), 291–331.

Naidu, S. (2014) "Crimes Against Nature: Ecocritical Discourse in South African Crime Fiction." *Scrutiny2*, 19(2), 59–70.

Nilsson, L. et al. (2017) "Introduction: Crime Fiction as World Literature." In L. Nilsson et al., eds., *Crime Fiction as World Literature.* New York: Bloomsbury, pp. 1–12.

Nixon, R. (2011) *Slow Violence and the Environmentalism of the Poor.* Cambridge, MA: Harvard University Press.

Parrinder, P. (2015) *Utopian Literature and Science: From the Scientific Revolution to Brave New World and Beyond.* London: Palgrave.

Pepper, A. (2016) *Unwilling Executioner: Crime Fiction and the State.* Oxford: Oxford University Press.

Pepper, A. and Schmid, D. (2016) "Introduction: Globalization and the State in Contemporary Crime Fiction." In A. Pepper and D. Schmid, eds., *Globalization and the State in Contemporary Crime Fiction: A World of Crime.* London: Palgrave, pp. 1–20.

Pezzotti, B. (2012) *The Importance of Place in Contemporary Italian Crime Fiction.* Madison, NJ: Fairleigh Dickinson University Press.

Piipponen, M. et al. (2020a) "From Mobile Crimes to Crimes of Mobility." In M. Piipponen et al., eds., *Transnational Crime Fiction: Mobility, Borders and Detection.* London: Palgrave, pp. 1–40.

Piipponen, M. et al. (eds.) (2020b) *Transnational Crime Fiction: Mobility, Borders and Detection.* London: Palgrave.

Polanski, R. (1974) *Chinatown.* USA: Robert Evans.

Poll, R. (2014) "The Rising Tide of Neoliberalism: Attica Locke's *Black Water Rising* and the Segregated Geographies of Globalization." In J. H. Kim, ed., *Class and Culture in Crime Fiction: Essays on Works in English since the 1970s.* Jefferson, NC: McFarland & Company, pp. 175–200.

Puxan-Oliva, M. (2020) "Crime Fiction and the Environment." In J. Allan et al., eds., *The Routledge Companion to Crime Fiction*. Abingdon: Routledge, pp. 362–370.

Puxan-Oliva, M. (2022) "Global Narrative Environments, or the Global Discourse of Space." In D. Roig-Sanz and N. Rotger, eds., *Global Literary Studies: Key Concepts*. Berlin: De Gruyter, pp. 37–60.

Rachman, S. (2010) "Poe and the Origins of Detective Fiction." In C. R. Nickerson, ed., *The Cambridge Companion to American Crime Fiction*. Cambridge: Cambridge University Press, pp. 17–28.

Rice, J. L. et al. (2021) "Against Climate Apartheid: Confronting the Persistent Legacies of Expandability for Climate Justice." *Environment and Planning E: Nature and Space*, 5(2), 625–645.

Riofrio, J. D. (2010) "When the First World Becomes the Third: The Paradox of Collapsed Borders in Two Novels by Gabriela Aleman." *MELUS (Multi-Ethnic Literature of the US)*, 35(1), 13–34.

Rustin, S. (2017) "Donna Leon: Why I Became an Eco-Detective Writer." *Guardian*, 15 April. Available at: www.theguardian.com/books/2017/apr/15/donna-leon-interview-commissario-brunetti-earthly-remains.

Schätzing, F. (2004) *Der Schwarm [The Swarm]*. Cologne: Kiepenheuer & Witsch.

Schmid, D. (2016) "The Bad and the Evil: Justice in the Novels of Paco Ignacio Taibo II." In A. Pepper and D. Schmid, eds., *Globalization and the State in Contemporary Crime Fiction: A World of Crime*. London: Palgrave, pp. 21–38.

Schneider-Mayerson, M. (2018) "The Influence of Climate Fiction: An Empirical Survey of Readers." *Environmental Humanities*, 10(2), 473–500.

Sharma, A. (2021) "Decolonizing International Relations: Confronting Erasures through Indigenous Knowledge Systems." *International Studies*, 58(1), 25–40.

Stević, A. and Tsang, P. (2019) "Introduction." In A. Stević and P. Tsang, eds., *The Limits of Cosmopolitanism: Globalization and Its Discontents in Contemporary Literature*. London: Routledge, pp. 1–9.

Stougaard-Nielsen, J. (2020) "World Literature." In J. Allan et al., eds., *The Routledge Companion to Crime Fiction*. Abingdon: Routledge, pp. 76–84.

Tillett, R. (2023) "Criminal Violences: The Continuum of Settler Colonialism and Climate Crisis in Recent Indigenous Fiction." In N. Ashman, ed., *The Routledge Handbook of Crime Fiction and Ecology*. New York: Routledge, pp. 282–294.

Trexler, A. (2015) *Anthropocene Fictions: The Novel in a Time of Climate Change*. Charlottesville: University of Virginia Press.

Tuomainen, A. ([2010] 2014) *The Healer.* Translated by L. Rogers. London: Vintage. Originally published in Finnish as *Parantaja.* Helsinki: Helsinki-kirjat.

Tyner, J. A. (2016) *Violence in Capitalism: Devaluing Life in an Age of Responsibility.* Lincoln: University of Nebraska Press.

VanderMeer, J. (2008) "The New Weird: It's Alive?" In A. VanderMeer and J. VanderMeer, eds., *The New Weird.* San Francisco, CA: Tachyon.

VanderMeer, J. (2021a) "13 Ways of Looking: Jeff VanderMeer." *Pioneer Works,* 9 April. Available at: https://pioneerworks.org/broadcast/13-ways-of-looking-with-jeff-vandermeer.

VanderMeer, J. (2021b) *Hummingbird Salamander.* London: 4th Estate.

Velie, A. R. (2009) "The Detective Novels of Qiu Xiaolong." *World Literature Today,* 83(3), 55–58.

Vidal-Pérez, A. (2023) "The Circulation of Global Environmental Concerns: Local and International Perspectives in the Verdenero Collection and Donna Leon's Crime Fiction." In N. Ashman, ed., *The Routledge Handbook of Crime Fiction and Ecology.* New York: Routledge, pp. 410–422.

Wagner Martin, L. (2012) *A History of American Literature: 1950 to the Present.* Chichester: Wiley Blackwell.

Walton, J. L. and Walton, S. (2018) "Introduction to Green Letters: Crime Fiction and Ecology." *Green Letters,* 22(1), 2–6.

Warnes, C. (2012) "Writing Crime in the New South Africa: Negotiating Threat in the Novels of Deon Meyer and Margie Orford." *Journal of South African Studies,* 38(4), 981–991.

Whyte, K. P. (2017) "Indigenous Climate Change Studies: Indigenizing Futures, Decolonizing the Anthropocene." *English Language Notes,* 55(1–2), pp. 153–162.

Wilson, J. (2021) "*Something New Under the Sun,* a Neo-Noir Set in an Even Thirstier Hollywood." *Vulture,* 2 August. Available at: www.vulture.com/article/something-new-under-the-sun-alexandra-kleeman-review.html.

Xiaolong, Q. (2012) *Don't Cry Thai Lake.* London: Hodder.

Žižek, S. (2003) "Parallax." *London Review of Books,* 20 November. Available at: www.lrb.co.uk/the-paper/v25/n22/slavoj-zizek/parallax.

Cambridge Elements ☰

Crime Narratives

Margot Douaihy
Emerson College

Margot Douaihy, PhD, is an assistant professor at Emerson College in Boston. She is the author of *Scorched Grace* (Gillian Flynn Books/Zando, 2023), which was named one of the best crime novels of 2023 by *The New York Times*, *The Guardian*, and *CrimeReads*. Her recent scholarship includes 'Beat the Clock: Queer Temporality and Disrupting Chrononormativity in Crime Fiction', a NeMLA 2024 paper.

Catherine Nickerson
Emory College of Arts and Sciences

Catherine Ross Nickerson is the author of *The Web of Iniquity: Early Detective Fiction by American Women* (Duke University Press, 1999), which was nominated for an Edgar Award by the Mystery Writers of America. She is the editor of *The Cambridge Companion to American Crime Fiction* (2010), as well as two volumes of reprinted novels by Anna Katharine Green and Metta Fuller Victor (Duke University Press).

Henry Sutton
University of East Anglia

Henry Sutton, SFHEA, is Professor of Creative Writing and Crime Fiction at the University of East Anglia. He is the author of fifteen novels, including two crime fiction series. His is also the author of the *Crafting Crime Fiction* (Manchester University Press, 2023), and the co-editor of *Domestic Noir: The New Face of 21st Century Crime Fiction* (Palgrave Macmillan, 2018).

About the Series

Publishing groundbreaking research from scholars and practitioners of crime writing in its many dynamic and evolving forms, this series examines and re-examines crime narratives as a global genre which began on the premise of entertainment, but quickly evolved to probe pressing political and sociological concerns, along with the human condition.

Cambridge Elements ≡

Crime Narratives

Elements in the Series

Printed in the United States
by Baker & Taylor Publisher Services